CH

Understanding
World History

The History
of Rock
and Roll

Other titles in the series include:

**Understanding
World History**

The History of Rock and Roll

Hal Marcovitz

**Bruno Leone
Series Consultant**

ReferencePoint Press®

San Diego, CA

© 2014 ReferencePoint Press, Inc.
Printed in the United States

For more information, contact:
ReferencePoint Press, Inc.
PO Box 27779
San Diego, CA 92198
www. ReferencePointPress.com

LIBRARY OF CONGRESS CATALOGING-IN-PUBLICATION DATA

Marcovitz, Hal.
   The history of rock and roll / by Hal Marcovitz.
     pages cm. -- (Understanding world history)
   Includes bibliographical references and index.
   ISBN-13: 978-1-60152-598-7 (hardback)
   ISBN-10: 1-60152-598-2 (hardback)
 1. Rock music--History and criticism. I. Title.
   ML3534.M349   2013
   781.6609--dc23

                                           2012049319

Contents

Foreword

When the Puritans first emigrated from England to America in 1630, they believed that their journey was blessed by a covenant between themselves and God. By the terms of that covenant they agreed to establish a community in the New World dedicated to what they believed was the true Christian faith. God, in turn, would reward their fidelity by making certain that they and their descendants would always experience his protection and enjoy material prosperity. Moreover, the Lord guaranteed that their land would be seen as a shining beacon—or in their words, a "city upon a hill,"—which the rest of the world would view with admiration and respect. By embracing this notion that God could and would shower his favor and special blessings upon them, the Puritans were adopting the providential philosophy of history—meaning that history is the unfolding of a plan established or guided by a higher intelligence.

The concept of intercession by a divine power is only one of many explanations of the driving forces of world history. Historians and philosophers alike have subscribed to numerous other ideas. For example, the ancient Greeks and Romans argued that history is cyclical. Nations and civilizations, according to these ancients of the Western world, rise and fall in unpredictable cycles; the only certainty is that these cycles will persist throughout an endless future. The German historian Oswald Spengler (1880–1936) echoed the ancients to some degree in his controversial study *The Decline of the West*. Spengler asserted that all civilizations inevitably pass through stages comparable to the life span of a person: childhood, youth, adulthood, old age, and, eventually, death. As the title of his work implies, Western civilization is currently entering its final stage.

Joining those who see purpose and direction in history are thinkers who completely reject the idea of meaning or certainty. Rather, they reason that since there are far too many random and unseen factors at work on the earth, historians would be unwise to endorse historical predictability of any type. Warfare (both nuclear and conventional), plagues, earthquakes, tsunamis, meteor showers, and other catastrophic world-changing events have loomed large throughout history and prehistory. In his essay "A Free Man's Worship," philosopher and

College Hill Library
http://www.westminsterlibrary.org
303-404-5555

Number of items:

1

Barcode:33020009951673
Title:The history of rock and roll /
Due:10/29/2019

10/8/2019   3:44 PM

Hours
M-W 9am-8pm
Th 9am-8pm
(IR) Th 9am-5pm
F 10am-5pm
(IR) F and Sat 10am-5pm
Sat and Su 1-5pm
(IR) Sun 1-5pm

. . .

mathematician Bertrand Russell (1872–1970) supported this argument, which many refer to as the nihilist or chaos theory of history. According to Russell, history follows no preordained path. Rather, the earth itself and all life on earth resulted from, as Russell describes it, an "accidental collocation of atoms." Based on this premise, he pessimistically concluded that all human achievement will eventually be "buried beneath the debris of a universe in ruins."

Whether history does or does not have an underlying purpose, historians, journalists, and countless others have nonetheless left behind a record of human activity tracing back nearly 6,000 years. From the dawn of the great ancient Near Eastern civilizations of Mesopotamia and Egypt to the modern economic and military behemoths China and the United States, humanity's deeds and misdeeds have been and continue to be monitored and recorded. The distinguished British scholar Arnold Toynbee (1889–1975), in his widely acclaimed twelve-volume work entitled *A Study of History,* studied twenty-one different civilizations that have passed through history's pages. He noted with certainty that others would follow.

In the final analysis, the academic and journalistic worlds mostly regard history as a record and explanation of past events. From a more practical perspective, history represents a sequence of building blocks—cultural, technological, military, and political—ready to be utilized and enhanced or maligned and perverted by the present. What that means is that all societies—whether advanced civilizations or preliterate tribal cultures—leave a legacy for succeeding generations to either embrace or disregard.

Recognizing the richness and fullness of history, the ReferencePoint Press Understanding World History series fosters an evaluation and interpretation of history and its influence on later generations. Each volume in the series approaches its subject chronologically and topically, with specific focus on nations, periods, or pivotal events. Primary and secondary source quotations are included, along with complete source notes and suggestions for further research.

Moreover, the series reflects the truism that the key to understanding the present frequently lies in the past. With that in mind, each series title concludes with a legacy chapter that highlights the bonds between past and present and, more important, demonstrates that world history is a continuum of peoples and ideas, sometimes hidden but there nonetheless, waiting to be discovered by those who choose to look.

Important Events in the History of Rock and Roll

1947
Rhythm and blues singer Roy Brown records the song "Good Rockin' Tonight," which becomes an important forerunner of the rock and roll sound.

1959
Rockers Buddy Holly, Ritchie Valens, and J.P. Richardson die in an airplane crash near Mason City, Iowa.

1929
Lester William Polsfuss, later known as Les Paul, jabs a phonograph needle into his acoustic guitar below the strings, wires it to an amplifier and speaker, and invents the electric guitar.

1954
Bill Haley and the Comets record "Shake, Rattle & Roll," the first major rock and roll hit.

1930   **1940**   **1950**   **1960**

1941
Paul develops the first solid-body electic guitar by attaching a guitar neck, bridge, and strings to a 4 x 4. Paul's design provides a more intense sound because the vibrations are not absorbed by the hollow acoustic guitar body.

1956
More than 60 million people tune in to *The Ed Sullivan Show* to watch a performance by Elvis Presley.

1951
Cleveland, Ohio, disc jockey Alan Freed premieres *The Moondog Show* on radio station WJW, specializing in jump blues. During one of the show's broadcasts, Freed coins the term *rock and roll*.

1953
Elvis Presley walks into Sun Records in Memphis, Tennesseee, to record two songs as a birthday gift for his mother. Sun executives soon sign him to a recording contract.

2012
The Rolling Stones mark their fiftieth anniversary by playing in front of sold-out venues in London, New York City, and Newark, New Jersey.

1964
The Beatles appear on American television for the first time when they perform live on *The Ed Sullivan Show*.

2006
Hip-hop stars Black Eyed Peas release the single "Pump It," in which they rap over the surf rock classic "Misirlou."

1963
The Beatles become international stars after releasing their first album, *Please Please Me*.

1977
Progressive rockers Emerson, Lake & Palmer tour with a seventy-piece orchestra providing their backup music.

1981
MTV premieres on the air. The first video broadcast by the new cable channel is "Video Killed the Radio Star" by the Buggles, a New Wave rock group.

1960   **1985**   **2010**

1960
Chubby Checker records "The Twist," establishing the twist as rock and roll's first homegrown dance.

1991
The grunge rock band Nirvana releases its most successful album, *Nevermind*.

1973
British rocker David Bowie releases the album *Aladdin Sane*, illustrating glam rock: The cover features Bowie's hair dyed red and styled into a mullet and his face painted with a red-and-blue zigzag pattern.

1969
In August, rock and roll bands use the Woodstock Music & Art Fair in upstate New York as a forum to protest the war in Vietnam; more than four hundred thousand fans attend the event.

The Defining Characteristics of Rock and Roll

Rock and roll legend Bruce Springsteen was asked what it is like to perform onstage in front of his fans. "Think of it this way," he responded. "Performing is like sprinting while screaming for three, four minutes. And then you do it again. And then you do it again. And then you walk a little, shouting the whole time. And so on. Your adrenaline quickly overwhelms your conditioning."[1] In answering the question, Springsteen summed up the essence of rock and roll: It is music that bursts with energy. Moreover, it can be loud and boisterous; it can be fun loving but occasionally angry. Romantic love is often the focus of the music, but rock and roll songs may also include politically charged and antiestablishment messages.

Springsteen made those comments while touring in 2012. When Springsteen and his group, the E Street Band, arrived in each city on the tour, they played to sold-out venues that seat thousands, and sometimes tens of thousands, of fans. Springsteen's fans epitomize typical rock fans—they have been dedicated to his music since he hit the rock scene in the 1970s; they know the lyrics by heart, they know the names of his bandmates, and they can cite, by memory, the important dates and releases in his career.

Americans were first introduced to the electrifying, high-energy, and often eardrum-shattering sounds of rock and roll long before Springsteen burst into stardom. Rock and roll emerged in the early

1950s. Its pioneer performers were influenced mostly by rhythm and blues, or R&B, a style of music played, at the time, largely by African American musicians.

Over the years, the term *rock and roll* has been used widely by fans, musicians, critics, and others to describe virtually all forms of pop music, whether it is performed by established rock musicians like Springsteen and the Rolling Stones or by pop divas like Katy Perry and Lady Gaga. The term *pop* is short for "popular," meaning that any song that gains traction with the public and enjoys big-time sales is regarded as a pop tune. Therefore, a lot of rock and roll music is pop music, but is all pop music rock and roll?

That is a question that has vexed experts since the dawn of rock and roll, mostly because rock and roll has never been easy to define. Says Roberto Avant-Mier, an author and professor of media studies at the University of Texas–El Paso, "A precise definition of rock is virtually impossible because of historical evidence that it does not confine itself to any one particular sound or style. . . . Rock music can probably be defined in terms of a point on a map with various intersections that collectively form some kind of nexus and the appearance of a location that could be called rock music."[2]

Playing It Loud

As rock music found its audience, its growth was helped along by technological developments—particularly the invention of the electric guitar and other amplified instruments, including keyboards and drum kits. One early and important development that helped bring about the rock and roll revolution was the transistor radio. Before electronics companies developed transistors—tiny components that amplify the electrical impulses that carry sound—radios relied on fragile glass vacuum tubes to perform that function. As such, most radios sat on tabletops in homes. But the development of the transistor in the 1950s meant radios could be made small, held in the hand, and taken anywhere by their owners—mostly teenagers. Indeed, young people were the first to recognize the overwhelming force of rock and roll music,

An exuberant Bruce Springsteen wows his audience during a 1984 concert. Like Springsteen, rock and roll music bursts with energy.

and transistor radios—which were also inexpensive—meant teenagers could take the music with them anywhere (preferably far away from their parents.)

Transistor radios were important to teenagers because at home, parents were likely to tell their sons and daughters to turn down the volume on their record players. A major characteristic of rock and roll is that it is played loud. Many dedicated rock fans believe that if the music is not loud, it is not true rock. "Music is an incredibly powerful medium to deliver a story by," says Eddie Vedder, lead singer and guitarist for the rock group Pearl Jam. "But the best thing is, you have to have volume. You're supposed to play it loud."[3]

The Diversity of Rock and Roll

Starting in the mid-1960s, rock and roll broke into its own subgenres: Among these categories are acid rock, heavy metal, glam rock, folk rock, and many others. They are all forms of rock music, but their sounds are very different. For example, fans of "head-banging" heavy metal bands such as Judas Priest and Black Sabbath are likely to have favored a different type of sound than fans who sought out the introspective, poetic folk rock of Simon & Garfunkel or those who pursued the angst-driven plaints of Nirvana.

Experts such as Jann Wenner, founder of *Rolling Stone* magazine, believe the beauty of rock and roll can be found in its diversity. Different sounds may appeal to different audiences, but in essence it is still all rock and roll. "When all is said and done, the story of rock and roll is the story of a sound. It is the sound of rural blues and folk instruments and voices, disseminated through the technologies of radio and records and eventually electrified," says Wenner. "It continues to grow and evolve."[4]

So when trying to put a label on rock and roll, listeners may find themselves challenged. The bottom line, though, is that rock fans listening to such contemporary groups as Foo Fighters, Arcade Fire, and Muse may not see the influences of early rock and roll performers such as Elvis Presley, Bill Haley, and Chuck Berry, but those pioneers have clearly left their mark on every guitar riff and drumbeat heard today.

Chapter 1

What Conditions Led to the Birth of Rock and Roll?

Back in the 1940s segregation was a fact of life in American society. Many public schools, buses and trains, theaters, restrooms, and other places were divided along racial lines. Music was segregated as well. Whites enjoyed the top swing bands of the era, led by bandleaders such as Artie Shaw and Benny Goodman. The singers who fronted these bands—among them Frank Sinatra and Bing Crosby—were almost always white. It was rare to find a black singer performing in front of a white swing band.

Denied these opportunities, blacks made their own music. By the late 1940s many African American music fans were dedicated to the rhythm and blues sounds of artists such as Louis Jordan, Big Joe Turner, Billy Right, and Roy Brown. This music was also known as jump blues because of its hard beat and fast-paced rhythm. In 1947 Brown recorded the song "Good Rockin' Tonight." The lyrics of the song tell the simple story of a young man in a hurry to meet his girlfriend so they can dance together and free themselves of their blues. It was the type of song that could get young people off their seats, clapping their hands, swinging their hips, and dancing.

It was also the type of song that listeners could find on Hunter Hancock's radio show in Los Angeles, California. Hancock played jazz, blues, and gospel music. He also played jump blues. Hancock's show appealed to African Americans. Advertisements for the program proclaimed, "The latest and greatest Negro performers and entertainers."[5]

Each day, listeners tuned in to hear Hancock shriek, growl, howl, and shout while introducing the songs, using the latest street slang as a way to connect with his audience. African American fans loved the music and Hancock's madcap style, but Hancock also had a lot of white listeners, particularly among the teenage population of the Los Angeles area. In fact, unknown to most of his listeners, Hancock was also white.

The Moondog Show

The fact that jump blues enjoyed a crossover appeal to young white music fans was also recognized by Leo Mintz, a record store owner in Cleveland, Ohio, who every day saw white teenagers in his store buying records cut by black jump blues performers. Mintz believed he could sell more records if more disc jockeys played rhythm and blues. So Mintz approached Alan Freed, a white disc jockey who at the time was hosting a classical music program on a Cleveland radio station. Mintz convinced Freed to host a show that would feature jump blues. "The beat is so strong anyone can dance to it,"[6] Mintz told Freed.

Freed agreed to host the show, and in June 1951 *The Moondog Show* premiered on radio station WJW in Cleveland. Freed borrowed the name of the show from the song "Blues for Moondog," which features a wailing saxophone solo he used each night to open his broadcast.

Freed did more than just spin records. He vocalized over the recordings as well, shouting "Go! Go! Gogogogogogogo!"[7] while thumping his hand hard onto a fat Cleveland phone directory to add percussion to his rants as the music played. Cleveland teenagers loved the sound, and soon Freed's show shot to the top of the Cleveland ratings. His show became so popular that in 1954 he moved to New York City radio station WINS, where he could find a much bigger audience. By then Freed had coined a new term for the music he played. He called it "rock and roll."

Tin Pan Alley

By the time Hancock, Mintz, and Freed discovered jump blues, most of American popular music was produced on West Twenty-Eighth Street in New York City, more commonly known as Tin Pan Alley. The origin of the nickname is unknown—it may have had something to do with the cacophony of sounds emanating from the myriad musical instruments in use on a typical day by composers and musicians. Or the street may have earned its nickname from the talent agents constantly banging on doors of music executives, trying to sell artists and songs as though they were street vendors seeking the attention of shoppers by banging hard on tin pans.

Whatever the origins of the name, some of the most talented songwriters of the first half of the twentieth century emerged from Tin Pan Alley, among them Irving Berlin, George and Ira Gershwin, George M. Cohan, and Cole Porter. These composers and lyricists would go on to write the hit songs of the era and later the music, lyrics, and librettos—the stories—for the first Broadway and movie musicals.

As with most of the rest of America, though, Tin Pan Alley was largely segregated: Few black singers or songwriters found success there. Among the exceptions were Scott Joplin, the most prominent composer of the genre known as ragtime, and Gussie Lord Davis, whose most popular Tin Pan Alley song was the romantic ballad "In the Baggage Coach Ahead," which was performed by a white singer, Imogene Comer.

The Chitlin' Circuit

Finding their paths to success through Tin Pan Alley mostly blocked by racial barriers, many black songwriters and musicians found other venues for their talents. During the 1920s many black artists turned to a new form of music known as jazz. Among the top performers of the early jazz era were Duke Ellington, Cab Calloway, Ethel Waters, Louis Armstrong, Lena Horne, Bill Robinson, and Billy Eckstine. Jazz performers played brassy melodies, and the lyrics were often based on bluesy and mournful stories. Improvisation was also key to the jazz sound: No two performances of the same song ever seemed to be the same. Jazz performers found their fans in the African American clubs of the era—venues such as the Cotton Club in New York, the Chocolate Bar and Hi Hat Club in Kansas City, and the Dreamland Ballroom and Pekin Theater in Chicago.

The roots of rock and roll can be found in many musical styles, including jazz. Among the influential jazz greats was trumpeter Louis Armstrong, whose carved wax image (pictured) stands in a Paris museum.

By the 1930s a new sound was emerging from the black music community. It was known as rhythm and blues, or more commonly as R&B. R&B found its voice on what was known as the Chitlin' Circuit—the neighborhoods in the cities of the South, Midwest, and mid-Atlantic states where African Americans made their homes. These neighborhoods had names like Little Harlem in New York City, Deep Ellum in Dallas, and the Third Ward in Chicago. In other cities many of these neighborhoods were simply called "Bronzeville." At night, their nightclubs burst with music from African American performers playing loud and raucous music.

"Back then you had big bands, anywhere from ten- to twenty-piece bands that had to squeeze themselves into a corner if there was no bandstand," recalls Sax Kari, a musician who played the Chitlin' Circuit for decades.

There were no inside toilets at many of these places; you had to use privies. Now, when you got into a place that had running water inside, why you were fortunate. They sold ice water. They didn't have air conditioners; they had these big garage fans: two on the bandstand and one back at the door. These were wooden buildings on the outside of town; there were very few concrete buildings or places in town. . . . We'd get the brass reeds on the back of the stage and get the drummer and rhythm section down front where you could see over their heads. You would play for two and a half hours straight, then take a thirty-minute break, then come back and play for the next hour and a half. Four-hour gigs."[8]

As with jazz, the music had a brassy sound—the instrument of choice in R&B was usually the saxophone. Unlike jazz, though, the lyrics of R&B often told a different story: Many R&B songs were upbeat and were just as likely to describe parties and good times as they were to tell of romances gone sour. It was this form of music that would eventually be refined by black musicians in the 1940s into jump blues and then into rock and roll by the musicians of the 1950s.

Teenage Audiences

In 1951 the black R&B band Kings of Rhythm, led by Ike Turner, released the single "Rocket 88." The song features a loud and rowdy beat as vocalist Jackie Brenston shouts the lyrics, which mainly speak to the singer's love for his hot new car. (The song is also credited to the band under the name Jackie Brenston and his Delta Cats.) Turner, Brenston, and their bandmates recorded the song in Memphis, Tennessee, at a new recording studio that had been established by Sam Phillips.

Phillips would soon emerge as one of the pioneers of rock and roll. In fact, Phillips regarded "Rocket 88" as the first true rock and roll song. Like a typical jump blues song, "Rocket 88" includes a lively beat, but the song takes jump blues a step further. For starters, the song features the sound of an electric guitar, which is not common in jump blues, where the saxophone is usually the predominant instrument. "If

Alan Freed and the Payola Scandal

After sitting atop the rock and roll world for more than a decade, the career of disc jockey Alan Freed came to a crashing halt in 1962 when he pleaded guilty to accepting $30,000 in bribes from record companies in exchange for plugging their songs on his show. The incident was known as the payola scandal—*payola* being a combination of the words *pay* and *Victrola*, which was the name of the original 1880s-era machine that played records.

According to music historian Irwin Stambler, payola was largely the reason rock and roll gained a foothold on the American airwaves. During the early years of rock and roll, Stambler says, many disc jockeys were hesitant to play the songs, fearing this revolutionary form of music would drive away their audiences. Record companies found that disc jockeys were much more receptive if they were offered cash bribes. "In effect, the rules . . . shut the industry doors to young writers and, to some extent, performers," Stambler says. "The answer that evolved was for the outsiders to find a new kind of music and then get it in the back door by paying off radio announcers to play it."

Freed was singled out for prosecution because he was the biggest name in rock and roll radio. After pleading guilty he was sentenced to pay a fine of just $300, but his career was ruined. He lived just three more years and died of kidney failure at age forty-three.

Irwin Stambler, *The Encyclopedia of Pop, Rock and Soul*. New York: St. Martin's, 1989, p. 243.

you listen to the music and the lyrics of 'Rocket 88,' it does all the right things at the right time," said Phillips. "To me, it's just an unbelievable crossroads that took place when I cut this darn thing."[9]

"Rocket 88" was an instant hit, thanks in large part to the airtime it received on Freed's show. The song found appeal among teenagers because it arrived at a time when attitudes among young people in America had started changing. Teenagers desired to break away from the influence of their parents, and one place where they could seek freedom was behind the wheels of their cars. By the 1950s cars were becoming more widely available and affordable, which meant teenagers could buy their own cars and soup them up, making them go faster. Songs like "Rocket 88" appealed to this rebellious side of American youth, and soon the song and others like it found audiences among white listeners—particularly young white listeners.

A Strong Backbeat

Certainly, another major reason for the appeal of rock and roll among young people is its beat, which is commonly played in what is known in music as 4/4 time. Under what musicians call a time signature, four beats are played in each measure (also known as a bar, the standard unit of notes in sheet music), and the basic note is a quarter note. This means the pace of the beat is quick, making it very danceable. Moreover, rock and roll has what is known as a strong backbeat, typically played by the drummer. In rock and roll, the drummer will pound hard on the second and fourth beats. Fans who follow along a rock and roll song by clapping their hands will find themselves clapping hardest on the second and fourth beats. In other words, a soft clap is followed by a hard clap, then a soft clap and finally a hard clap—that is the rock and roll backbeat, which helps enhance the music's appeal to dancers.

Rock and roll also came to be defined by the instruments used by its musicians, and no instrument defines rock and roll more than the electric guitar. Says *Rolling Stone* senior editor David Fricke, "Rock and roll has been the sound of ecstasy, change and independence for more than half a century. And the guitar is still its defining instrument, because of its endless capacity for shock and challenge—the determination to get a piece of that freedom and rapture for yourself, turn it up and take it further."[10]

Rock and roll fans have a guitar player from Waukesha, Wisconsin, to thank for the invention of the electric guitar. Born in 1915, Lester

Many music historians regard "Rocket 88" as the first true rock and roll song. But the song also enjoys another special place in rock history: It is the first rock and roll song to sing the praises of the American automobile. Many others followed. Among them are "Little Deuce Coupe" by the Beach Boys, "Go Lil' Camaro Go" by the Ramones, "Little GTO" by Ronny and the Daytonas, "Dead Man's Curve" by Jan and Dean, "Mercedes Benz" by Janis Joplin," and "Pink Cadillac" by Bruce Springsteen.

Pioneer rock and roll record producer Sam Phillips, whose Sun Records released "Rocket 88" in 1951, recalled that he recognized the song's hit potential specifically because it spoke to the appeal of hot cars to young people. "I knew how much young people loved the idea of having some wheels," Phillips said. "They had been so denied, it was hard to get even a tire during [World War II]. After the war, people began to have some halfway normal relationship with the automobile. If you had a car, it was just a symbol that, 'Boy, I'm grown up.' It hasn't changed today."

Quoted in Gerri Hirshey, "Pink Cadillacs, Little Red Corvettes: Paradise by the Dashboard," *Rolling Stone*, May 11, 2000, p. 87.

William Polsfuss took piano lessons as a young boy and was such a mediocre student that his teacher warned his mother that her son had no ear for music. "Your boy, Lester, will never learn music,"[11] the teacher wrote in a letter to Polsfuss's mother.

But the boy persisted and soon taught himself to play the harmonica, banjo, and guitar, buying his first acoustic guitar from the Sears, Roebuck catalog for $2.49. As a teenager he spent hours listening to the radio and imitating the sounds of the guitar players whose shows were broadcast from the nearby city of Chicago. He also liked to tinker with gadgets—particularly electrical gadgets—a hobby that would soon lead to a great innovation.

Arrival of the Electric Guitar

By age fourteen Polsfuss's talents as a musician had progressed to the point that he was able to earn money by playing professionally, performing under the name Red Hot Red. Polsfuss played country-and-western music, finding his talents mostly in demand for church socials, fraternal organization meetings, cafés, and speakeasies—the illegal saloons that went into business during the 1920s following the adoption of the Eighteenth Amendment to the US Constitution, which outlawed alcohol sales.

The speakeasies were invariably crowded and noisy, and Polsfuss often found it difficult to make his voice and guitar heard above the din. And so one night in 1929, he arrived at a show in Goerke's Corners, Wisconsin, bringing along his acoustic guitar as well as his father's combination radio-phonograph player. He removed the needle from the phonograph arm and jammed it into the wood beneath the guitar strings. Next, he ran a wire from the needle to the radio's amplified speaker. And so when Polsfuss strummed the strings, the needle picked up the vibrations and transmitted them through the speaker. Polsfuss's crudely wired concoction provided extra volume for the guitar and enabled the instrument to be heard over the noisy crowd. As Polsfuss played for the speakeasy crowd in Goerke's Corners, his electrically amplified guitar gave the music a metallic sound, and he could turn up the volume as high as the dial on the amplifier would go. This loud and metallic sound would become a distinctive element of rock and roll.

More than eight decades later, the basic concept of the electric guitar has not changed. Instead of a phonograph needle, modern guitar makers employ a magnetic bar wrapped in wires that carries electrical current. When the strings are plucked, the vibrations are picked up by the magnet and transmitted through a wire to an amplifier, which boosts the sound and transmits it through speakers.

Hunter Hancock, the white disc jockey credited with introducing jump blues to a wide audience in Southern California, drifted into radio after a lifetime spent in aimless jobs. By the time he was twenty-five, Hancock estimated he had held twenty-two jobs, including bank clerk, chauffeur, and vaudeville singer. In 1943 he found a job as a Sunday disc jockey on radio station KFVD in Los Angeles.

Hancock played mostly jazz to a small audience but his ratings shot up in 1947 when a salesman for a record store asked him to play rhythm and blues records. "In no time the show was a hit," Hancock recalled. "The station sold so many commercials that they had to add another half-hour, then yet another hour, until I was finally doing three-and-a-half hours every day, Monday through Saturday."

Few listeners knew that Hancock was white, but that changed in 1955 when Hancock hosted a TV show on Friday nights called *Rhythm and Bluesville*. Hancock's show featured a mix of rhythm and blues and rock and roll artists who performed live. Among the guests on the show were rocker Little Richard as well as R&B star Fats Domino.

Hancock left radio in 1968 after his station changed to a pop format, meaning Hancock was unable to play the music of R&B and pure rock he loved so well. "I had to spin a lot of records that I was frankly ashamed to play," he said. Hancock died in 2004 at the age of eighty-eight.

Quoted in Eric Olsen, "R&B Radio Pioneer Hunter Hancock Dies," Blogcritics.org, August 12, 2004. http://blogcritics.org.

Les Paul and the Log

By the 1930s Polsfuss had changed his name to Les Paul and was touring the Midwest with a country-and-western combo. His contribution to the development of the electric guitar—and ultimately, rock and roll—did not end when he jammed a phonograph needle into the body of his acoustic guitar. In 1941 Paul was living in New York City and playing guitar for a swing band. Still tinkering with electrical gadgets, Paul approached Epi Stathopoulo, owner of the Epiphone Guitar Company, and won permission to use Stathopoulo's factory to tinker with some designs for a new guitar he had in mind.

Paul took a length of 4 x 4 lumber and fitted it with strings, a bridge, and two electrical pickups. He gave it a standard guitar shape by attaching "wings" to the sides made from scraps he found around the factory. He called the device the "log," but in reality Paul had invented the first solid-body electric guitar. The music it produced was much fuller than the sounds produced by the amplified acoustic guitars Paul had been using. Because the strings were attached to a solid body rather than a hollow acoustic instrument, the strings produced far more intense vibrations than what could be produced on the acoustic guitar. Moreover, the solid body did not absorb the vibrations the way hollow guitars tended to do, which further intensified the sound.

Paul recalled that his new instrument was met with a measure of hostility from established musicians. "Most players were dead set against the electric guitar," he said. "Violinists said it sounded 'barbaric,' horn players didn't like it either because they couldn't compete with a volume knob, and guitarists said it was a novelty with no lasting value. I argued with the musicians' union in every city to list me as an electric guitarist, but they wouldn't accept it as a separate instrument."[12]

Soon, though, other musicians and musical instrument companies were adopting Paul's idea, and in 1948 musician and inventor Leo Fender developed his own version of the solid-body electric guitar. Other guitar companies raced to catch up with Fender. One of these was the Gibson Guitar Company; in 1951 the company asked Paul to help design an electric guitar. The guitar produced from the

Les Paul's invention, the electric guitar, provided the signature sound of rock music. One of Paul's designs, the 1955 Gibson Les Paul Goldtop guitar, is pictured.

collaboration between Paul and Gibson would become standard equipment during the 1950s as rock and roll groups established themselves on the music scene.

In fact, Gibson named its first electric guitar the "Les Paul." In the coming years rock and roll bands would routinely employ other electrically amplified musical instruments, including drum kits equipped with microphones as well as electronic keyboards. But since the dawn of rock and roll, it has been the electric guitar player who stands in front onstage. Says historian André Millard, "The amplified guitar sound—the distinctive crash of the power chord or the screeching whine of distortion—is the signature of rock 'n' roll."[13]

"Rock Around the Clock" Conquers the World

One musician who used a Gibson electric guitar was Bill Haley, leader of a rock and roll band known as Bill Haley and the Comets. In 1952 Haley and his group recorded "Crazy Man, Crazy" for a small Philadelphia-based independent label, Essex. The song was a modest hit and helped Haley and his band sign a recording deal with a much bigger label, Decca. In 1954 the group recorded a major hit for Decca, "Shake, Rattle & Roll." The song would chalk up sales of more than 1 million, earning Haley and his band a gold record. At the time, most teenagers bought 45s—7-inch (18 cm) vinyl records that cost less than one dollar. The 45s—so named because they spun on the record turntable at forty-five revolutions per minute—featured two songs, one on the A side and one on the B side. Typically, the A side was the more popular song, and the B side featured a lesser-known song by the performer.

"Shake, Rattle & Roll" owed no small measure of its success to Freed as well as other disc jockeys who by now had discovered the enormous popularity of rock and roll among teenage listeners. The song received heavy airplay on the radio, but later in 1954 another single recorded by Haley's group would enjoy even more success. The song was titled "Rock Around the Clock." Soon after its release, the song zoomed to the top of the charts. On July 9, 1955, the song was listed in the top spot on the *Billboard* magazine chart and held its place there for the next eight weeks. Over the next six decades the popularity of "Rock Around the Clock" has never ebbed, and it remains a hot seller even in the MP3 age. According to *Rolling Stone*, since it was first released as a 45, "Rock Around the Clock" has sold at least 25 million copies, making it one of the best-selling songs of all time.

The song's lyrics simply invite listeners to get onto the dance floor and rock at all hours of the day and night. The song illustrates what rock and roll is all about: Dancing, good times, and a carefree attitude that teenagers could readily embrace. Says author and rock historian Jim Dawson, "The real beginning of rock 'n' roll as a phenomenon was July 2, 1955, when 'Rock Around the Clock' climbed to the pinnacle of American pop charts in the July 9 issue of *Billboard* magazine and heralded the arrival of the youth culture that eventually conquered the world."[14]

By the time Bill Haley and the Comets recorded "Rock Around the Clock" in 1954, rock and roll music had come a long way in the three short years since Freed first went on the air with *The Moondog Show*. Helped along by visionaries such as Hunter Hancock, Leo Mintz, and Les Paul, the music evolved from jump blues, a genre favored mostly by African American listeners, to rock and roll, a genre enjoyed universally by young people of all races.

Chapter 2

Rockabilly, Duck Walking, and the Death of Buddy Holly

Elvis Presley grew up in the small town of Tupelo, Mississippi. By 1953 he was living in Memphis, Tennessee, and working as a truck driver when he walked into the studio of Sun Records. Eighteen years old at the time, Presley paid for studio time out of his own pocket. Self-taught as a singer and guitar player, he intended to record two ballads as a birthday gift for his mother.

By then Sun Records founder Sam Phillips was searching for talented singers and musicians who could produce what Phillips called "rockabilly"—a hybrid of country music and R&B played to a rock and roll beat. During the 1950s Phillips found several singers who could produce the sound he wanted—among them Carl Perkins, Roy Orbison, and Jerry Lee Lewis—but no other singer discovered by Phillips would achieve stardom on the scale reached by Presley.

A talented singer and incandescent performer, Presley brought sex appeal to rock and roll as he performed with his hair styled in a pompadour and his sideburns cut long. It was the way he swiveled his hips, though, that sparked the most reaction from audiences and prompted critics to nickname him "The Pelvis." While witnessing a Presley concert, *Los Angeles Times* reporter Wally George was stunned by the adoration heaped on Presley by the audience—mostly by the teen-age girls in attendance. "It was not the music that sold them," George wrote. "It was his hips. They wiggled, they bumped, they twisted."[15]

Close-Knit Family

Growing up in Depression-era Tupelo, Presley and his parents, Vernon and Gladys, lived through difficult times. Both parents found little work during the 1930s. Moreover, the Presleys suffered a tragedy when Elvis's twin brother, Jesse, died at birth. And in the late 1940s, Vernon served a brief jail sentence in a fraud case. But the Presleys were a close-knit family, sticking by one another during difficult times. They were also a churchgoing family as well, meaning every Sunday morning Elvis was exposed to gospel music. Meanwhile, at home, country-and-western music played on the Presley family radio. These were the sounds that Presley heard and grew to love as he was growing up and learning about music. For his thirteenth birthday, his parents gave him a guitar.

By the time he walked into the Sun Records studio five years later, Presley was hardly a naive country boy. After moving to Memphis, he discovered Beale Street, where most of the city's R&B nightclubs were located. Saving the money he earned as a truck driver, Presley bought himself a suit of what he called his "cat clothes"—pink shirts with wide collars, black slacks, jackets with padded shoulders, and shiny leather shoes and boots. As for the music he heard on Beale Street, Presley had become a devoted fan of jump blues.

Back in the 1950s, anybody could walk into Sun Records, pay three dollars, and cut their own 45. Presley paid the fee and recorded two songs in the Sun studio: "My Happiness" and "That's When Your Heart-aches Begin" as a birthday gift for his mother. They were both moody R&B songs made famous by the African American group the Ink Spots.

Phillips's secretary, Marion Keisker, listened to Presley's performance and played a tape of the session for her boss. Phillips was initially unimpressed, but months later he heard a song he liked, "With-out You," and wanted to record a version of it at Sun. At that point,

Elvis Presley, pictured performing in 1968, helped make rockabilly a national phenomenon. But it was his onstage swagger—the famous Presley hip gyrations—that most excited his many adoring fans.

Keisker urged Phillips to give Presley an audition. Phillips agreed and summoned Presley to the studio. As things turned out, the song produced from that session was not "Without You" but a bluegrass song,

"Blue Moon of Kentucky," played to a rock and roll beat. The song enjoyed modest success when Phillips sold it as a 45, but a few months later Presley recorded the Roy Brown jump blues song "Good Rockin' Tonight," which garnered considerably higher sales and helped launch Presley toward stardom.

Onstage Swagger

Presley's first true hit for Sun Records was "That's All Right (Mama)," released in 1954. As the record started climbing the charts, Sun Records booked its new star for performances in front of live audiences. It was during these early days of performing live that Presley perfected his onstage swagger along with his hip gyrations, which gave his act a dose of sex appeal. "Elvis, instead of just standing there flat-footed and tapping his foot, well, he was kind of jiggling. . . . Plus, I think those old loose britches that we wore—they weren't pegged, they had lots of material and pleated fronts—you shook your leg, and it made it look like all hell was going on," recalled guitarist Scott Moore, who played behind Presley onstage. "During the instrumental parts he would back off from the mike and be playing and shaking, and the crowd would just go wild."[16] As for Presley, he told a reporter after one performance, "I did a little more, and the more I did, the wilder they went."[17]

"That's All Right (Mama)" helped launch rockabilly into a national phenomenon. Lacking the brassy wail of the saxophone found in most jump blues music, rockabilly helped set rock and roll apart from R&B, giving it a unique sound dependent on the guitarists, vocalists, and percussion instruments.

Throughout the remainder of the decade, Presley would go on to record a series of hit songs, including "Heartbreak Hotel," "Don't Be Cruel," "Hound Dog," "Love Me Tender," "All Shook Up" and "Jailhouse Rock." Presley made his national television debut in 1956 when he performed on *Stage Show*, which was hosted by swing era band leaders Tommy and Jimmy Dorsey. The show was a hit, garnering an 18 percent rating, meaning 18 percent of the nation's television sets were tuned in to the performance. Even bigger TV audiences were in store as Presley soon appeared on shows hosted by comedians Steve Allen and Milton Berle.

In September 1956 Presley found his biggest audience to date when he appeared on *The Ed Sullivan Show* in front of a TV audience estimated at 60 million people—a truly astounding number because at the

Elvis and the "Colonel"

Elvis Presley was Sun Records' biggest star, but Sun was a small operation that its owner, Sam Phillips, often had trouble keeping afloat. In 1955, to stave off bankruptcy, Phillips was forced to sell Presley's contract to RCA Records for $40,000. Phillips, who gave RCA all of Presley's tapes, received $35,000 in the deal while Presley received $5,000.

It was a paltry payoff for Presley, but his deal with RCA would soon prove to be very lucrative—Presley would go on to make tens of millions of dollars. Soon after leaving Sun, he recorded such huge hits as "Don't Be Cruel," "Heartbreak Hotel" and "Hound Dog." Presley was also cast for roles in Hollywood movies—a career move that came about thanks to the wheeling and dealing of Presley's new manager, Tom Parker. Parker preferred to be called the "Colonel," although he had served only briefly in the military and had never achieved the rank of colonel. In fact, Parker was an illegal immigrant—he had sneaked into the country from the Netherlands. (His real name was Andreas Cornelius van Kujik.)

Despite his dubious background, Parker's skills as a talent promoter helped make Presley into an international superstar. His fee was substantial—while most entertainment managers accepted 10 percent of their stars' salaries as payment, Parker demanded 50 percent of Presley's earnings—a fee Presley never questioned throughout his long career.

time, the number of American homes with TV sets numbered fewer than 25 million. This meant that whole families had gathered around their TV sets that Sunday night to watch this phenomenal performer spread the message of rock and roll.

The "Killer" Arrives

Phillips hoped to match Presley's success with other rockabilly stars in the Sun Records stable. He came closest with Jerry Lee Lewis. Growing up in Ferriday, Louisiana, Lewis would often sneak away from home at night and steal across town to Haney's Big House, a nightclub where black R&B musicians performed. As with most of the rest of the South, Ferriday was a segregated town in the 1940s, so Lewis, who was white, could no more walk into Haney's and enjoy the music than a black person could take a seat in a roadhouse in the white section of town. He listened to the music from his hiding place just outside the building.

Lewis learned to play the piano and soon realized music was his best hope to escape life in Ferriday. At home, his religious parents, Elmo and Mamie, demanded that he play gospel music. Jerry Lee was so talented that Elmo hefted the piano onto the back of the family's pickup truck and drove to camp meetings and church services, where his son played gospel music for churchgoers. But when Elmo and Mamie were not home, Jerry Lee imitated the sounds he heard while hiding behind Haney's.

When Lewis turned fourteen his parents sent him to the Southwestern Bible Institute in Waxahachie, Texas, with the notion that their boy would study for the ministry. Always something of a hellraiser—his nickname was "Killer"—Lewis snuck out of the dormitory at night and hitchhiked to nearby Dallas, where he went to the movies or dances or snuck into nightclubs to listen to jump blues performers. Back in Waxahachie he cut classes, preferring instead to spend hours at the piano. When a school official caught him playing the gospel hymn "My God Is Real" with a jump blues rhythm, he was kicked out. Lewis had lasted three months in Waxahachie.

The Doo Wop Sound

During the 1950s rock and roll stars often found themselves competing for top places on the popular music charts with stars of a form of music known as doo wop. As with rock and roll, doo wop traces its roots to the R&B sounds pioneered by black artists a decade before, among them the Ink Spots and the Mills Brothers.

Doo wop relied more on vocals than electrically amplified instruments. It was often performed a cappella—without instrumental accompaniment. And instead of lyrics, the vocals often imitated the sounds of the instruments. "'Doo wop' is a term that had redefined blending of classic R&B, with vocal group harmonies, street corner singers, falsetto leads, baritone and bass singers whose deep voices could simulate any musical instrument," says T.J. Lubinsky, who hosts a nationally broadcast doo wop radio show.

A major star of the doo wop era was Gene Vincent, whose first hit, "Be-Bop-a-Lula," which he recorded in 1956, was a typical doo wop song. As with rock and roll, doo wop crossed color lines. Other big doo wop stars included white performers such as Dion and the Belmonts and the Skyliners, while black doo wop groups included the Drifters, Frankie Lymon and the Teenagers, and Little Anthony and the Imperials.

Quoted in "Cousin Brucie" Morrow and Rich Maloof, *Doo Wop: The Music, the Times, the Era*. New York: Sterling, 2007, p. 13.

Slamming Out the Notes

Lewis spent the next decade as a piano player for hire, providing backup music mostly for country-and-western performers. In 1957 Lewis arrived in Memphis and learned Sun Records was in need of a session pianist. He got the job and soon found himself playing in the backup combo for a record cut by Perkins. After listening to Lewis's work for Perkins and other Sun performers, Phillips decided Lewis could be a major talent.

Phillips scheduled a recording session for Lewis, who performed a song he had heard two years before—"Whole Lotta Shakin' Goin' On." It is a rousing, fast-paced song that tells a story about a hot party in a barn. Sun released the song as a single, and it quickly shot to the top of the charts. Just by listening to the song, fans could tell that Lewis brought a lot of energy to his music—but when they saw him perform the song in person, they got a dose of energy and talent they had never envisioned.

Lewis was invited to perform "Whole Lotta Shakin' Goin' On" on television's popular *Steve Allen Show*. When he took the stage, Lewis did a lot more than just sit at the piano and play the song. Soon after the song started, Lewis stood at the keyboards and kicked the piano stool away. Shouting the lyrics, he brought his hands down hard on the keys, slamming out the notes. And then he raised a leg over the keyboard and banged out the notes with his heel. The studio audience had never seen anything like it and shrieked with delight. Lewis was now one of rock and roll's biggest stars.

By now the old guard of the music world was divided on rock and roll. When Gene Austin, one of the first of the swing band crooners, was asked what he thought of rock and roll, he huffed, "I've been around the music business a long time, and I think I know something about how it works and how trend follows trend. All this rock-n-roll business is going to fade soon."[18] But Bing Crosby liked what he heard. "When a rock rhythm section gets its beat going good, and its loud electric guitar thumping, it doesn't give up; it's inexorable," Crosby said. "It gives off a beat so strong you can walk on it. After a while you start tapping your foot, and if you're young you want to dance."[19]

The Duck Walk

The rockabilly played by Presley and Lewis was rock and roll, but the music also drew sounds from country and western—a genre of music most popular in the southern states. Rock and roll would grow in popularity in other parts of the country as performers from the cities of the North and Midwest refined the sound, influencing the music with their own styles. One of the pioneers who introduced rock and roll to urban audiences was Chuck Berry.

Born in St. Louis, Missouri, in 1926, Berry learned to play the guitar but treated music as a hobby more than a career path. An African American, Berry enjoyed jazz and swing music but found himself inspired mostly by the soulful sounds of the blues. Berry first heard the sounds of blues musicians on the radios owned by inmates in reform school, where he spent three years after foolishly taking part in a robbery. By 1950 he was out of reform school, married with two children, and working as a hair stylist when he started playing professionally to help supplement his income. He formed a trio with two other St. Louis musicians. By 1955 Berry and his bandmates found themselves in demand by the black nightclubs in the city. Moreover, Berry was also writing many of the trio's songs.

One of those songs was titled "Maybellene." The song tells the story of a hot rod race and broken romance and was written to a rock and roll beat. Berry took his electric guitar and the sheet music for "Maybellene" and several other songs to Chicago, where he sought out blues legend Muddy Waters. Waters listened to Berry play the guitar and, impressed with his talent, recommended him to Leonard Chess, the president of Waters's label, Chess Records. In 1955 Chess recorded Berry performing the song. "Maybellene" was an instant hit, and it led to stardom for Berry as he followed up that song with other hits, including "Roll Over Beethoven (and Dig Those Rhythm & Blues)" and "Johnny B. Goode."

As with Lewis and Presley, Berry proved that in rock and roll, stage presence was as important as the music. Berry had always found a way to dance while performing, wielding his electric guitar as though it were his partner, but in 1956 at a concert at the Paramount Theatre in Brooklyn, New York, Berry unveiled a new dance move. He called it the duck walk. Bending at the knees, he plucked out the notes on his guitar as he strode across the stage, hunched over but with a fluidity of movement that left the audience awestruck. The duck walk would become his signature movement as the flamboyant performer turned into a rock superstar.

Sequins and Cardigans

Berry's style may have awed rock and roll fans, but during the 1950s no rock and roll performer matched Little Richard for sheer flamboyance.

The music of Little Richard (pictured) was loud, electric, and energetic. He was also one of the most flamboyant rock and roll musicians of the 1950s.

Born Richard Penniman in 1932 the African American singer and pianist's early career was confined to black nightclubs. Still a teenager in the late 1940s, he played in R&B combos and swing bands, but as rock and roll became popular in the 1950s he embraced the sound and started composing his own songs. Little Richard's music was loud, electric, and energetic, and the lyrics often did not seem to matter. One of his first big hits, "Tutti Frutti," contained the lyrics "A womp-bompaloo bompalompbompbomp."[20] Onstage, fans saw a performer who dressed in sequins and capes and wore his hair straightened and greased into a pompadour.

Of course, rockers did not have to wear sequins or perform duck walks to find fans. In 1958 New York–born Bobby Darin scored a major rock and roll hit with the song "Splish-Splash." The song's lyrics were typical for the era, essentially telling the story of a young man in search of a hot party. Also a songwriter, Darin is reported to have written the song in just twelve minutes.

Onstage, Darin hardly resembled Presley, Lewis, Berry, or Little Richard. Instead, fans found the performer to be a young, clean-cut singer usually dressed in a suit or cardigan sweater. Despite the demure dress, Darin could still belt out rock and roll. "He was very secure, very confident, very gifted," recalls Neil Sedaka, a songwriter and performer who during the 1950s was getting his start in popular music as a piano player. "He knew he was going to be a star. He played me 'Splish-Splash' before it came out . . . and I said, 'Oh my god, that is sensational."[21] "Splish-Splash" was, however, the highlight of Darin's rock and roll career. He soon dropped rock for a pop-jazz sound and then pursued an acting career.

The Death of Buddy Holly

As the 1950s came to a close, rock and roll established itself as a major force in the world of entertainment. But in 1959 a tragic event occurred that delivered a devastating blow to the world of rock. On February 3 Buddy Holly, one of rock and roll's rising stars, died in a plane crash while on his way to a performance. Also killed in the crash were two other stars:

The Death of Buddy Holly in Song

Buddy Holly's death was recounted in the 1971 hit song "American Pie" by folksinger Don McLean. Although McLean has always been vague about the meaning of the lyrics, he acknowledges that he wrote the song as a tribute to Holly. "He was the person that made me learn the guitar," McLean says. "I loved the way he played and thought for a while that I might dig playing rock 'n' roll, but by the time I was 18 I was deeply into folk music."

The song, which spans more than eight minutes, covers the history of rock and roll through the early 1970s, with references to stars such as the Beatles, Monotones, Bob Dylan, the Rolling Stones, and Janis Joplin. But the song's most well-known lyrics— "The day the music died"—are, according to rock historian Irwin Stambler, a direct reference to the crash of Holly's plane on February 3, 1959. In 2001 a survey sponsored by the Recording Industry Association of America, the trade group of the record industry, and the National Endowment for the Arts, selected "American Pie" for fifth place on the list of greatest pop songs of the twentieth century.

Quoted in Irwin Stambler, *The Encyclopedia of Pop, Rock and Soul.* New York: St. Martin's, 1989, pp. 455–57.

Ritchie Valens, one of the few Hispanic rock and roll performers of the era, and J.P. Richardson, a singer, songwriter and disc jockey known as the "Big Bopper" who recorded the novelty hit "Chantilly Lace."

But it was the death of Holly that shook rock and roll fans the most. The sound Holly developed with his band, the Crickets, would have an enormous impact on rock and roll in the coming years. Before the Crickets started recording music, in most rock songs the lead electric guitar provided the major instrumental sound while the backup guitar players added complementary sounds. But Holly and fellow Crickets guitarist Niki Sullivan played their instruments in sync, giving the music a fuller sound and more energy. Among the hits recorded by Buddy Holly and the Crickets were "Peggy Sue," "That'll Be the Day," and "Oh, Boy."

The plane crash occurred as Holly, Valens, and Richardson were touring cities in the Midwest. Weary from weeks of travel, Holly and the others hired a small plane in Mason City, Iowa, to fly them to their next gig in Fargo, North Dakota, while their bandmates made the trip by bus. The plane took off in a blinding snowstorm and soon crashed, killing all aboard.

In just a few years, top groups such as the Beatles and Rolling Stones would base their sound on the music of the Crickets. Says rock and roll historian Bruce Eder, "In a career lasting from the spring of 1957 until the winter of 1958–1959 . . . Holly became the single most influential creative force in early rock and roll."[22]

At the start of the 1950s, rock and roll had just emerged on the music scene, but by the close of the decade it was the dominant sound in popular music. The ascent of rock and roll was aided by the sex appeal of Presley as well as the flamboyance of stars such as Lewis, Berry, and Little Richard. But these stars and others proved the music also had substance and could stand on its own merits, giving less flamboyant performers such as Darin and Holly a chance to shine.

Chapter 3

The 1960s Rock Metamorphosis

Ernest Evans had twice tried to break into rock and roll by recording singles for the Philadelphia, Pennsylvania–based record label Cameo. Neither of the songs, titled "The Class" and "Dancing Dinosaur," managed to break into the charts, but there was no denying Evans's talent. Growing up in a tough neighborhood in South Philadelphia, Evans learned to sing on street corners, where he gathered with friends to sing the songs they heard on the radio a cappella—without instrumental accompaniment. To support himself, Evans worked in a street-side butcher stand, plucking chickens.

Evans did not perform under his true name but adopted the stage name Chubby Checker. The stocky Evans picked the name as something of a gag. He hoped his stage name would help him garner attention among fans of the popular R&B pianist and singer Fats Domino.

In 1960 producers at Cameo asked Checker to record a song titled "The Twist." Another group, Hank Ballard and the Midnighters, had released the song a year before, but Ballard's recording failed to find an audience, and the song soon disappeared from the airwaves. "The Twist" invites listeners to get up on their feet and dance. Checker brought a robust energy to his performance, which helped propel "The Twist" into first place on the rock and roll charts. As the song gained in popularity, it seemed everyone in the country was doing the twist. Checker was invited to perform the song on *The Ed Sullivan Show*, making his appearance in October 1961. "The Twist has added electricity, giving show business a shot in the arm,"[23] Sullivan declared after Checker's appearance.

Rock Gets Its Own Dance

The popularity of the twist marked a milestone in the young history of rock and roll. Rock and roll was very danceable music, to be sure, but it had never before had a dance of its own. There had been other attempts made at establishing a true rock and roll dance—in 1959 R&B singer James Brown recorded "(Do the) Mashed Potatoes," which introduced the dance mashed potato. The song was a hit, but the mashed potato took some talent to master—it required a lot of coordinated heel, toe, and knee movements.

The twist was far easier: Most anyone could do it. Twisters need only stand in place and swivel their hips, knees, arms, and trunk in time to the beat. "There are no basic steps in the Twist," Checker explained. "You move chest, hips and arms from side to side and balance on the balls of the feet."[24]

Other dance crazes would follow. Soon performers recorded songs inviting people to frug, watusi, swim, monkey, and jerk. Some of these songs were hits, but none have had the staying power of the twist. In 2008 *Billboard* magazine marked its fiftieth anniversary by naming the song "The Twist" number one among the top one hundred rock and roll songs to have appeared on the magazine's charts.

Dancing on *American Bandstand*

To learn how to do the twist, one had to *see* the twist. The popularity of the song was helped along when Checker appeared on Sullivan's show, but the TV program that first gave the song and dance widespread exposure was *American Bandstand*. The program, which aired daily Monday through Friday, was produced locally by a Philadelphia-based TV station, WFIL, and carried nationally on the ABC television network. It was broadcast in the late afternoon, a time when teenagers were home from school and able to watch the program before dinner.

American Bandstand remained on the air from 1952 through 1988. For much of the show's run the host was Dick Clark, who would emerge as an enormously influential figure in rock and roll and other genres of pop music. Record producers anxious to hype their records

The *American Bandstand* Committee

Producers of *American Bandstand* sought to ensure that only clean-cut, well-behaved young people danced on the show. A strict dress code was enforced: Boys had to wear jackets and ties, girls were required to wear skirts or dresses. And no tight, hip-hugging clothes were allowed. To enforce the dress code, and to make sure all the teenagers remained on their best behavior while in the studio, the producers established a committee of a dozen dancers to act as mentors and role models for the other cast members. According to committee member Jerry Blavat, the main job of the group was to ensure that everyone got along. "There were no rivalries," he says. "We were all friends."

For the dancers, it was important to gain the favor of the committee. Members of the committee selected the dancers who participated in the daily "Rate-a-Record" segment. Each day, Clark called over two dancers, played a record, and asked them to comment on the song and assign it a numerical score. The segment was important to performers and producers because it provided important exposure for their songs—and they naturally hoped the young dancers would like the music and give it high marks. But "Rate-a-Record" was also an important segment for the dancers, because it ensured they would be featured on camera—which was, after all, the ultimate goal for all *American Bandstand* dancers.

Quoted in John A. Jackson, *American Bandstand: Dick Clark and the Making of a Rock 'n' Roll Empire.* New York: Oxford University Press, 1997, p. 22.

appealed to Clark to feature their performers on his show. During the early years of *American Bandstand*, rock and roll stars booked on the show included Ike Turner, Roy Orbison, and Jerry Lee Lewis, as well as doo wop groups Dion and the Belmonts and the Drifters and R&B stars Jackie Wilson and Fats Domino.

American Bandstand was more than just an opportunity for singers and groups to perform their hits in front of a camera. The studio was set up as a dance floor, and during each program local teenagers—handpicked by the show's producers—danced to the music performed on the bandstand. The cameras did not stay focused on the performers onstage; instead, they often zeroed in on the dancers. During the late 1950s and early 1960s, Arlene Sullivan and her partner Kenny Rossi were regular members of the *American Bandstand* dance cast. Sullivan recalls:

> It got to the point where the regular kids wanted to be on camera all the time, so Dick Clark would turn off the red light [on the camera] so we were supposed to not know which camera was on. But we always knew where the camera was. We were hams. . . . You knew how they were focusing. And then Dick Clark would start to say, if he thought we were in front too long, "OK, Arlene and Kenny in the back, Franni in the back, Carole in the back." He wanted to give the other kids a shot.[25]

In time, audience members at home watched the show as much to see the dancers as the performers. The teenagers developed dedicated fans who hoped to see their favorite *Bandstand* dancers each day. *Teen* magazine sent reporters to Philadelphia to write feature stories on the dancers; in 1960 the magazine published two special issues, each spanning eighty pages, devoted entirely to the *Bandstand* dancers.

Regardless of how popular the dancers may have been among the teenagers watching at home, the show still provided rock and roll artists—both rising and established—an important audience for their music. Checker performed "The Twist" on *American Bandstand* on September 29, 1960—nearly a year before his appearance on the Sullivan show. "Being on *Bandstand* was like getting a Nobel Prize," says Checker. "From 3 o'clock in the afternoon until 5 o'clock, nobody was on the street. They were watching *Bandstand*. Can you imagine that?"[26]

The British Invasion

As Americans were doing the twist and watching *American Bandstand*, interest in rock and roll had now reached across the Atlantic Ocean. In working-class Liverpool, England, two young musicians, John Lennon and Paul McCartney, formed a rock and roll band. They labored in small clubs in England as well as other European cities under various names, among them the Quarrymen, Black Jacks, and Silver Beetles. By 1963 they were known as the Beatles, and their other bandmates were George Harrison and Ringo Starr. That year, the Beatles released the album *Please Please Me*, which shot to the top of the charts and made the Beatles into international celebrities, particularly after they appeared on Sullivan's show for three consecutive appearances in February 1964.

When the Beatles arrived in New York for their Sullivan show appearances, they kicked off a trend in rock and roll known as the British Invasion. They were followed by other British groups also pursuing stardom in America—among them the Rolling Stones, the Dave Clark Five, the Animals, Freddie and the Dreamers, and Herman's Hermits.

But the Beatles were by far the top British band to cross the Atlantic, and in fact, for much of the 1960s they were the top rock and roll band in the world. On the evening of August 15, 1965, the Beatles—by now dubbed by the press the "Fab Four"—strode onto a stage that had been set up in the infield of Shea Stadium, at the time the home of the New York Mets. Every seat in the stadium was occupied: When promoters announced plans for the event, tickets sold out within minutes. When the music started it seemed to *New York Times* reporter Murray Schumach that the noise from the thousands of Beatles fans in the stands easily drowned out the music made by the Fab Four. Schumach wrote in his story about the concert:

> Their immature lungs produced a sound so staggering, so massive, so shrill and sustained that it quickly crossed the line from enthusiasm into hysteria and was soon in the area of the classic Greek meaning of the word pandemonium—the region of all demons.

The sound was accompanied by weeping, stamping, leaping, weaving—and in dozens of cases, fainting—by adolescent girls.[27]

Some fifty-five thousand fans attended the concert. At the time, the Shea Stadium event featuring the Beatles set a record for rock concert attendance.

When the Beatles and other British bands found fans in America, most homegrown rockers were clean-cut American boys like Frankie Avalon, Ricky Nelson, Fabian, and Bobby Rydell. They wore crew cuts or carefully styled hair held in place by gels and tonics. When the Beatles arrived in America, they introduced a long and unkempt hairstyle to the American public. As the Beatles rose in popularity, their "mop tops" were soon adopted by millions of teenage boys. As young people adopted the Beatles' hairstyle, the *New York Times* reported:

Where once the crew cut reigned supreme, today the object is to retain as much hair as possible, especially over the eyes. The bang's the thing, at best barely clearing the brows, at worst looking as if it had been chewed off by bears. To the barber it means a minimum of comb and cut; to the Beatles devotee it's "boss," in the same class as tight pants, loud music and the right not to bathe; to the parent, it is to suffer.[28]

Bad Boys of British Rock

The Beatles may have shocked parents with their haircuts, but the songs they played in the early and mid-1960s were largely inoffensive. Mostly the group recorded songs about boy-meets-girl romantic love, such as "She Loves You," "I Want To Hold Your Hand," and "I Saw Her Standing There." But another British group gaining a large following in America was releasing far edgier music, establishing a reputation as the bad boys of British rock. The band was known as the Rolling Stones. The group's lead singer was Michael Phillip Jagger—"Mick" to his fans—a former student at the prestigious London School of Economics. Other original members of the group included Keith Richards,

The British rock invasion began with the Beatles, shown arriving in California in 1964. The group was the top British band to cross the Atlantic and for much of the 1960s they were the top rock band worldwide.

Brian Jones, Bill Wyman, Ian Stewart, and Charlie Watts. The Stones started playing together in 1962 and made their American debut in June 1964, touring nine cities in the span of two weeks.

As with the Beatles, the Stones could sing about romantic love, but there was often a darker side to their music. Among the group's hits were "Honky Tonk Woman," which told of a drunken fling in a dingy barroom; "Brown Sugar," a story about the rape of a young black slave girl; "Paint It, Black," in which a spurned lover seeks to blacken out all images of life; and "Under My Thumb," a song that finds the protagonist proclaiming that he is now the boss over his girlfriend. Other Stones hits included "(I Can't Get No) Satisfaction," in which the singer laments the dead ends in his life; "Jumping Jack Flash," which tells the story of a young man's mental and physical abuse; and "Sympathy for the Devil," in which Satan takes credit for the ills that plague the world.

The stories told by the songs were far removed from the rock and roll tunes that had been popular in the prior decade. It was hard to imagine critics raising complaints about the lyrics of "Rock Around the Clock" or "Tutti Frutti," but when the Stones released "Let's Spend the Night Together" in 1967 many voices were raised in protest. In the song, the singer asks his girlfriend for premarital sex, a topic that was regarded as taboo in the era. When the Stones were rehearsing the song for an appearance on *The Ed Sullivan Show*, Sullivan heard the lyrics and demanded they be changed to "Let's spend some time together." The Stones agreed, but Jagger still sang the song with a dose of sultriness that appalled many critics. "The Rolling Stones," huffed *Washington Post* columnist Mopsy Strange Kennedy, "have . . . personal dirtiness, lyric sexiness, questionable morals [and] a generally rapist aura that some teenagers find appealing in their heroes."[29]

However, other critics found much to like about the Stones, arguing that the group's edginess gave rock and roll a new dimension. Wrote rock critic Geoffrey Cannon, "The Stones are perverted, outrageous, violent, repulsive, ugly, tasteless, incoherent. A travesty. That's what's good about them."[30]

Bikinis, Folksingers, and Drugs

As many rock and roll fans were learning, though, the hard rocking and often dark sound favored by the Rolling Stones was only one variety of rock and roll. By the mid-1960s rock and roll had branched out into many subgenres. For example, one of the most popular rock sounds of the era was so-called surf music. These songs were usually played hard

Jimi Hendrix: The Greatest Rock and Roll Guitarist

Jimi Hendrix was one of the brightest rock stars of the 1960s. Born in Seattle, Washington, Hendrix was drawn to R&B as a teenager. After serving in the US Army, Hendrix found work as a backup guitarist for a number of R&B groups, but in 1966 he switched to hard rock and formed his own group, the Jimi Hendrix Experience. Over the next four years, he recorded a number of hits, including "Purple Haze," "Hey Joe," and "All Along the Watchtower." Perhaps the highlight of his career occurred at the Woodstock Music & Art Fair in 1969. Hendrix closed the show—and the opening song in his set was a hard-rocking, electrified version of "The Star-Spangled Banner."

Hendrix's music was popular among drug users, who believed his long guitar solos enhanced the hallucinogenic effects of psychedelic drugs. Nevertheless, there was no denying his talent: In 2012 *Rolling Stone* magazine named Hendrix the greatest guitar player in rock history. "He made the electric guitar beautiful," says Pete Townshend, guitarist for the Who. "It had always been dangerous, it had always been able to evoke anger. . . . Jimi made it beautiful, and made it OK to make it beautiful."

Hendrix rocked hard, but he also partied hard. He died of a drug overdose in 1970. He was just twenty-seven years old.

Pete Townshend, "Jimi Hendrix," *Rolling Stone Special Edition*, 2012, p. 10.

and fast, with the sound dominated by the electric guitar, but the topics of the lyrics invariably centered on fun in the sand, surfboards, and girls in bikinis. Among the major performers of the surf era were Jan and Dean and the Beach Boys.

Formed in 1961, the Beach Boys scored a modest hit a year later when they released their debut album *Surfin' Safari*. "I remember hearing Surfin' Safari first when I was in sixth grade," says Lindsey Buckingham, guitarist for the pop-rock group Fleetwood Mac. "It had the beat, the sense of joy, that explosion rock and roll gave to a lot of us. But it also had this incredible lift, this amazing kind of chemical reaction that seemed to happen inside you when you heard it."[31]

Members of the Beach Boys included brothers Brian, Dennis, and Carl Wilson as well as a cousin, Mike Love, and two friends, Al Jardine and David Marks. The album features songs punctuated by heavy guitar sounds while the lyrics tell of the laid back life of the California teenager. "We had a very unique sound with those rock and roll guitars," says Marks. "And Brian's beautiful vocal harmonies and his arrangements with the rock guitars created something that people hadn't really heard before. It was a new sound that was very unique at the time. There was a wide opening. There just wasn't very much happening then."[32]

The band followed up *Surfin' Safari* with an even bigger hit the next year: *Surfin' USA*. The album's title track reached number two on the 1963 *Billboard* magazine chart and remained on the chart for more than a year. The lyrics of "Surfin' USA" as well as the other tracks on the album entice listeners with the same type of lifestyle the group's earlier songs promoted: sand, surf and sun. Says Buckingham, "The Beach Boys showed the way, and not just to Californians."[33]

During the 1960s women started coming into their own as rockers, thanks largely to the efforts of record producer Phil Spector, who discovered girl groups such as the Ronnettes and the Crystals. The Ronnettes' biggest hit, "Be My Baby," earned the group a gold record in 1963. Several female stars were part of the British Invasion—they included Petula Clark, Dusty Springfield, and Marianne Faithfull. But the hardest-rocking woman of the 1960s was Janis Joplin, who belted out lyrics in a throaty and often mournful wail. Joining the group Big Brother and the Holding Company in 1965, Joplin recorded hits such as "Summertime," "Piece of My Heart," "Ball and Chain," and "Down on Me."

By the mid-1960s one of the most popular stars in American music was folksinger Bob Dylan, who had a dedicated fan base thanks to hits such as "Mr. Tambourine Man," "The Times They Are a-Changin'," and "Blowin' in the Wind." When Dylan "went electric" in 1965—trading his acoustic guitar for an electric guitar—he drew much criticism from his fans but, nevertheless, helped launch the genre of folk rock.

And as drug use became more prevalent in the 1960s, acid rock

Women rockers, including Janis Joplin, established their own reputations in the 1960s. Joplin, pictured in concert in 1968, was known for belting out lyrics in a throaty and often mournful wail.

gained many fans. The music performed by artists such as Jefferson Airplane, Jimi Hendrix, and the Grateful Dead was believed to enhance the experience of tripping on lysergic acid diethylamide, known on the street as LSD or acid. Acid rock includes long, improvised guitar solos that drug users believe help emphasize the hallucinogenic effects of psychedelic substances.

Protest Music

As folk rock, acid rock, and other subgenres of rock and roll dominated the charts, many rock performers found themselves in opposition to the Vietnam War and used their music to voice their attitudes about the conflict. During the 1960s, as the war raged in Southeast Asia, opposition to the war was led by college students and other young people. They demonstrated against the conflict as well as the draft that forced them to serve in the armed services and participate in a war in which they did not believe. Eventually, the Vietnam War protest movement culminated in 1969 at the Woodstock Music & Art Fair in upstate New York, where many rock stars performed songs with antiwar messages before an audience of some four hundred thousand young fans.

Among the most popular antiwar songs of the late 1960s were "Eve of Destruction" by Barry McGuire, "I Feel Like I'm Fixin' to Die Rag" by Country Joe and the Fish, "For What It's Worth" by Buffalo Springfield, and "Fortunate Son" by Creedence Clearwater Revival. Following the Woodstock festival, singer and songwriter Joni Mitchell wrote the song "Woodstock," in which the protagonist dreams jet bombers he sees in the sky turn into butterflies. The song was recorded by folk rockers Crosby, Stills, Nash & Young.

Writer Mikal Gilmore believes that rock music provided young people with their most effective voice as they protested the war. Because of its widespread popularity, rock music could serve as a resource to spread an antiwar message that young people could not find in other media. Says Gilmore, "[When] President Lyndon B. Johnson began actively committing American troops to a highly controversial military action in Vietnam . . . it quickly became apparent that it was the young

Acid rock gained fans as drug use became more prevalent in 1960s America. Musicians such as Jimi Hendrix (shown performing in 1970) became known for long, improvised guitar solos that were thought to heighten the hallucinogenic effects of psychedelic drugs.

who would pay the bloodiest costs for this lamentable war effort. Sixties rock had given young people a sense that they possessed not just a new identity, but a new empowerment."[34]

Woodstock may have closed the 1960s, but American involvement in the war ground on until 1975. During the early 1970s performers such as John Lennon ("Imagine"), Elton John ("Daniel"), and Crosby, Stills, Nash & Young ("Ohio") continued recording songs protesting the war and advocating peace.

The 1960s began with Chubby Checker inviting everybody to get off their feet and twist. During the decade, rock and roll went through a complete metamorphosis. By the dawn of the 1970s, people were still dancing to rock and roll music, but the sound had reached across an ocean, finding in Great Britain a wealth of rock and roll talent. During the 1960s women discovered they could create rock music as well. And as the decade progressed, people would come to associate the music with edgy lifestyles, drug use, and the political empowerment of a generation of young people who found that rock and roll could provide them with a powerful voice.

Chapter 4

Rock Enters the Video Age

Anybody attending a Devo concert in the 1970s would find a much different style of rock music than they were used to hearing from the Beatles or Rolling Stones. For starters, to produce its sound, Devo relied heavily on the synthesizer, an electronic instrument controlled by a keyboard that could imitate other instruments such as the guitar, organ, or even drums. When played by Devo member Gerald Casale, the synthesizer added a sound that gave the music something of a technical flavor, as though it had been concocted at a computer keyboard rather than written by penning notes onto the staffs of sheet music.

The musicians of Devo did not sound like the Beatles or the Stones—and they did not look like them either. They performed in yellow nylon costumes, wearing kooky hats resembling flower pots turned upside down. Lead singer Mark Mothersbaugh shouted the lyrics to the band's songs in short, staccato bursts. Moreover, the band members moved about the stage in carefully choreographed motions—jumping about and twisting their bodies in sync.

Despite the weirdness, many rock critics liked what they heard and saw. *Los Angeles Times* rock critic Richard Cromelin believed Devo's sound mirrored the culture from which it emerged—a society just discovering the power and complexity of the digital age. "Devo is among the first wave of rock bands to root an experimental approach in gut-level reality," suggested Cromelin. "The fact that its vigorous, intense show also qualifies as marvelous entertainment is an added bonus. Whether it's enough to break through rock's obvious values remains to be seen."[35]

Strange New Territories

Devo was part of a movement in rock and roll known as New Wave. The name was taken from the New Wave movement in filmmaking that started in France in the 1950s when directors used experimental techniques—such as unorthodox camera angles, choppy film editing, and improvised dialogue—to tell their stories. By the 1970s many musicians were anxious to push rock and roll into strange, new territories. Devo, with its outlandish costumes, tightly choreographed stage presence, and music produced by synthesizers, was one of the founders of the New Wave movement in rock.

Another New Wave group was the Buggles, a British duo composed of Trevor Horne and Geoff Downes. The two singers formed the group in 1979, made two albums, then broke up in 1980. They did score one modest hit, however: "Video Killed the Radio Star," which sold well in Europe. American rock fans were introduced to the Buggles not through the sound of their music but through a video produced for their hit song. Indeed, the airing of the video for "Video Killed the Radio Star" represents an important milestone in the history of rock and roll—as well as all popular music in America—because it was the first video aired on a new cable TV channel that went live on August 1, 1981. At 12:01 a.m. that morning, Music Television—known more commonly as MTV—debuted when an announcer spoke the words, "Ladies and gentleman, rock 'n' roll."[36] Those words were followed by a brief film of a rocket lifting off from a launch pad and then the video of the Buggles' song.

The video shows Horne and Downes traipsing through an eerie collection of old TV sets, radios, and jukeboxes while a confused little girl wanders through the scene. Selection of the video for the network's launch showed that the MTV executives had a sense of humor. They believed strongly that video would not kill the rock and roll stars of the radio era and, instead, that the launch of their channel would help revolutionize the music industry. Alan Hunter, one of the first MTV veejays—the on-camera hosts who introduced the videos—watched MTV's first televised images with other veejays as well as network

The Playful Side of Rock and Roll

Rock lyrics usually dwelled on serious themes of love, war, and teen angst, but many rock musicians also had a playful side. In 1962 Bobby "Boris" Pickett released the novelty hit "Monster Mash." The song was a spoof of the novel *Franken-stein*, in which a scientist creates life in the laboratory, but in Picket's version the monster jumps off the slab and starts rocking. Three years later, Sam the Sham and the Pharaohs recorded "Wooly Bully," a song about two young people inspired to dance after seeing a buffalo. And in 1966 the Royal Guardsmen recorded "Snoopy vs. the Red Baron," based on the *Peanuts* comic strip character Snoopy and his imaginary battles against the German World War I flying ace Manfred von Richthofen.

Ray Stevens recorded a hit in 1969 titled "Gitarzan," based on the stories of the jungle king Tarzan. In Stevens's version Tarzan is the guitar-playing leader of a rock and roll band that features his girlfriend Jane and a monkey on vocals.

One of the biggest hits of 1973 was "Cover of the *Rolling Stone*" by Dr. Hook and the Medicine Show. In the song, band members sing of their widespread success but wonder why—with all their money, adoring fans, and hit records—the editors of *Rolling Stone* steadfastly refuse to feature the band on the cover. On March 29, 1973, *Rolling Stone* relented and published a caricature of the band on the magazine's cover.

technicians. He says, "After the Buggles came on we all just looked at each other and said . . . 'This might just get big.'"[37]

Some rockers resisted the video age at first, believing it was a passing fad that cheapened the quality of their art. The heavy metal band Metallica was among the groups that at first refused to produce videos for their music. "It was discussed, and it was thrown out. It was re-discussed, and it was thrown out again," says Martin Hooker, head of Music for Nations, Metallica's label. "Music video was suddenly the thing, everybody had to do a video, but Metallica were the exception to the rule. . . . It just meant that the band were even more in demand live, because that was the only way people were going to see them."[38]

The Buggles' video may have launched MTV but it was far from the first music video to have been produced. In fact, the music video was born six years prior to the launch of MTV when the TV show *Midnight Special* featured a six-minute video of the song "Bohemian Rhapsody" by Queen. Few people probably saw that history-making moment; although broadcast nationally on the NBC television network, *Midnight Special* aired from 12:30 to 2:00 on Saturday mornings. Soon, though, other music-oriented TV shows started airing videos. As videos became an integral part of the music business, many top bands realized they would not only have to record their sounds but find ways to dramatize the music in a visual format.

Glam Rockers and Hair Bands

Queen, the band whose video launched it all, grew out of the glam rock movement that found favor among many fans during the 1970s. It was British rocker David Bowie, though, who was the foremost star of glam rock, also known as glitter rock. In glam rock the look was as important as the music; the glam rock stars wore outrageous costumes and wild hair styles suggesting an androgynous stage presence. The cover of Bowie's 1973 album *Aladdin Sane* provides a typical illustration of the glam rock look: The album cover features a photo of Bowie with his hair dyed red and styled in a mullet and a red-and-blue zigzag pattern painted across his face.

Glam rock came and went rather quickly, but some glam rockers, including Elton John and Queen, proved very successful. And after the glam rock fad passed, Queen, John, and Bowie kept their careers relevant by dropping the glittered costumes and going for a more mainstream rock sound in their music.

British rocker Elton John, performing in 1986, exemplified glam rock's affinity for outrageous costumes and wild hair styles. Unlike that of some glam rockers, John's music has endured.

Glam rock was just one of the new subgenres of rock and roll that appealed to fans in the 1970s and 1980s. Starting in the 1970s the heavy metal sound attracted big audiences. In addition to Metallica, other major heavy metal bands of the era included Judas Priest, KISS, and Black Sabbath. Heavy metal features electric guitar riffs played to the loudest degree, their sounds often as distorted as they are amplified. Meanwhile, drums are banged with reckless abandon while the singers deliver the lyrics charged with emotion. Some metal bands included glam elements and were also known as hair bands because the performers wore their long hair coiffed into fancy styles and dyed pink, purple, or other outlandish colors.

The Punks and Progressive Rockers

There was nothing glam, however, about punk rock—another genre that emerged in the 1970s. Among the leaders of the punk movement in rock were the Sex Pistols, the Clash, and the Ramones. Punk rock is angry music—the songs were decidedly antiestablishment as punkers denounced the standards of polite society and proclaimed they would live by their own rules. The music could be vulgar, but for fans of the genre vulgarity was at the center of its appeal. Roger Sabin, a college lecturer in cultural studies in Great Britain, says:

> We can say that punk was/is a subculture best characterized as being part youth rebellion, part artistic statement. . . . It had its primary manifestation in music—and specifically in the disaffected rock and roll bands like the Sex Pistols and the Clash. Philosophically, it had no "set agenda". . . but nevertheless stood for identifiable attitudes, among them: an emphasis on negativism . . . a consciousness of class-based politics (with a stress of "working class credibility"); and a belief in spontaneity and "doing it yourself."[39]

Punk rock had its dedicated following, but some punk groups were able to move beyond the genre and find wider audiences. The Police started out as a punk band but moved on to a more mainstream sound, recording melodic tunes more reminiscent of the Beatles than the Clash. The band's lead singer, Gordon Sumner—known as Sting—became a sex symbol as the group grew beyond punk to record romantic ballads such as "Every Breath You Take" and "Wrapped Around Your Finger."

While some fans stayed loyal to the vulgarity of punk and others preferred a softer side from groups such as the Police, some rock fans were far more interested in the sound of the music than its meaning. These fans could be found at concerts featuring bands playing progressive rock. Progressive rock bands relied more heavily on instrumentation and less on vocals—top performers were Emerson, Lake & Palmer, the Moody Blues, and Pink Floyd. The tracks on progressive rock albums could span as much as ten or twenty minutes. Indeed, Emerson, Lake & Palmer's albums always featured long solos by keyboardist

Rise and Fall of the Sex Pistols

No punk group personified its genre more than the British band the Sex Pistols. Two of the band's performers assumed decidedly antiestablishment stage names: John Lydon took the name Johnny Rotten, and John Ritchie preferred to be known as Sid Vicious. (Other members were Steve Jones and Paul Cook.) Formed in 1975, the Sex Pistols often performed shirtless and sang of anarchy; poked fun at "God Save the Queen," the national anthem of Great Britain; accused the police of brutality; and trivialized the Holocaust—the extermination of European Jews by the Nazi regime.

By 1978 the band had broken up. Lydon embarked on a solo career, and Ritchie suffered an addiction to heroin. On October 12, 1978, Ritchie was charged with the murder of his American girlfriend, Nancy Spungen. Released on bail, Ritchie was found dead on February 1, 1979, the victim of a drug overdose. In 1986 the rise and fall of the Sex Pistols and the relationship between Spungen and Ritchie was dramatized in the film *Sid and Nancy*.

Keith Emerson. Moreover, Emerson was a big fan of the American classical composer Aaron Copland and adapted Copland's music, including "Fanfare for the Common Man" and "Hoedown," to rock instruments and a rock beat. In 1977 the trio toured with a seventy-piece orchestra providing their backup music. "What we're trying to do is to move on from wailing guitars and 'my baby's left me,'" said guitarist and vocalist Greg Lake. "You can only do that so long before it becomes utterly meaningless. We're using the orchestra because we felt our music could move forward through it."[40]

Motown

As rock grew with the sounds of progressive rock, punk rock, and the other genres, other forms of music gained in popularity as well. During the 1960s and 1970s, R&B found a huge audience thanks mostly to the Detroit-based label Motown, founded by producer Berry Gordy Jr. Gordy signed stars such as Smokey Robinson and the Miracles, Diana Ross and the Supremes, Stevie Wonder, and the Temptations. Motown also introduced music fans to five brothers performing under the name the Jackson 5. The youngest of these brothers—just six years old when he made his debut with the group—was Michael Jackson.

R&B was given a big boost with the production of the TV show *Soul Train*, which first went on the air in 1970. The show went into national syndication a year later and remained in production until 2006. Soul Train was hosted by Don Cornelius, a former police officer who went into broadcasting after a radio executive complimented him on his deep, baritone voice—as Cornelius issued him a traffic ticket.

Soul Train was essentially *American Bandstand* for R&B fans. As with *Bandstand*, the studio was filled with young dancers who performed to recorded music or the sounds of R&B artists making guest appearances. Each week, a highlight of the show featured the Soul Train Dancers forming two rows. Pairs of dancers would then take their turns strutting down the center, showing their best dance moves, as they approached the camera.

The Disco Sound

Pop music exploded in the 1960s and 1970s as well. Not really rock and roll or R&B or any other genre in particular, pop is at its core lively and danceable music performed by singers and bands who have found widespread and devoted audiences. No pop music movement had a bigger impact on the 1970s than disco—thanks to the enormous popularity of the film *Saturday Night Fever* and its soundtrack album. Many of the songs for the film were performed by Australian brothers Barry, Robin, and Maurice Gibb, known to their fans as the Bee Gees. Other big stars of the disco era were Donna Summer, Gloria Gaynor, Kool & the Gang, the Village People, and Van McCoy, who recorded "The Hustle"—arguably the signature dance song of the disco era.

But it was the Gibb brothers who ruled the disco world. During the 1960s and 1970s the Bee Gees were the hottest pop act in Australia. In 1977 producer Robert Stigwood asked the brothers to write the songs for a movie he was developing about the disco scene in New York City. Starring TV actor John Travolta, *Saturday Night Fever* would go on to gross more than $230 million in worldwide ticket sales. The film opens as Travolta, who plays paint store clerk Tony Manero, walks the streets of the city as the Bee Gees give voice to the peppy signature song of the film, "Stayin' Alive."

A New Generation of Stars

Disco would die out by the early 1980s, replaced by a new generation of pop stars who, thanks to the popularity of MTV and other music video channels, could showcase their singing, dancing, and acting abilities. Many of these performers proved to be very telegenic: Among them were Michael Jackson, his sister Janet Jackson, Madonna, the Go-Go's, Blondie, Olivia Newton-John, Cyndi Lauper, the Pointer Sisters, the Bangles, Wham!, and Paula Abdul. The 1980s also saw the launch of hip-hop music when early rappers such as Ice-T, N.W.A., 2 Live Crew, the Beastie Boys, and Public Enemy cut their first albums.

As the pop stars and rappers saw their careers rise, in no small part due to their embrace of the medium of music videos, mainstream rockers found themselves with no choice but to join the video revolution as well. Holdouts such as Metallica relented and made videos. During the 1980s rockers such as Prince, Culture Club, Van Halen, and Guns N' Roses found their success had a lot to do with the number of times their videos played on MTV. A rock video produced in 1986, "Sledgehammer" by Peter Gabriel, was selected by *Rolling Stone* for first place on its list of top one hundred videos of all time. Using pioneering computer animation effects, the surreal video features Gabriel performing the song as various weird effects occur on the screen: Gabriel's head turns into a vegetable; later a locomotive circles his head and a group of chickens dance through the scene.

Grunge Rock Makes a Statement

Pop and hip-hop are far removed from the rock of Chuck Berry, Bill Haley, and Buddy Holly, but it could be argued that all these forms of music share similar traits. After all, R&B led to rock and roll, but R&B also led to the style of music known as funk, which many music experts find at the roots of rap. Funk emerged in the late 1960s and early 1970s as an electrified mix of R&B, soul music, and jazz. During the 1970s DJs in urban clubs started making their own mixes of recorded funk tunes—a technique known as sampling—then added rhymed poetry in time with the beat. And there have been occasions when rap music has borrowed directly from rock and roll. In 2006 the Black Eyed Peas released the single "Pump It," rapping over the rock guitar music of "Misirlou," a surf classic first recorded in 1962. Meanwhile, pop music may lack a hard rock beat, but most pop singers perform as electric guitars and other amplified instruments provide the backup sounds.

As pop and hip-hop challenged rock and roll for popularity, rock musicians found new ways to reach their fans. During the 1990s grunge rock found a wide audience among young people known as Generation X. Members of the generation who reached their teenage years and young adulthood in the 1990s were the sons and daughters of the baby boomers, the generation born during the two decades following the end of World War II. The baby boomers created and managed the society in which this new generation had come of age; indeed, the president for much of the decade, Bill Clinton, was a baby boomer. What was left for this new generation of Americans to accomplish? For Generation X—or Gen X—the answer was, not much. Many Gen Xers felt unchallenged by life ahead. They had been raised in prosperous times and were now living in a society that they had played no role in shaping. Opportunity had been handed to them—too easily, many thought. Many members of Gen X felt a deep sense of angst over their circumstances.

And that was the message delivered through the music of the rock bands that put voice to the unhappiness of Gen X. Centered largely in the Seattle, Washington, area, grunge rock found a wide audience among Gen-Xers as bands such as Pearl Jam, Stone Temple Pilots, and Alice in Chains recorded major albums during the 1990s, capturing the sour moods of their fans. No band, however, captured that angst more fully than Nirvana, led by troubled singer and guitarist Kurt Cobain. In 1991 Nirvana released its most successful album, *Nevermind*, whose title seemed to say it all—the word illustrated Cobain's attitude toward life. Moreover, the top single from the album, "Smells like Teen Spirit," includes mournful lyrics in which Cobain vocalizes his generation's desire to accomplish nothing with their lives. The song's video features the band performing in a smoky high school gymnasium; as Cobain wails out the lyrics, and as lazy cheerleaders wave their pom-poms with little enthusiasm, the teenagers sitting in the grandstand turn into an unruly mob—all clearly embracing Cobain's message. "*Nevermind* was an album crammed full of angst, inner struggle, and contempt for the society," says Latoya Peterson, a writer for *Spin* magazine. "As song after song from the album entered heavy rotation on the radio and MTV, Nirvana reached millions of people who saw themselves as outcasts."[41]

Among the members of Gen X, perhaps no one was filled with as much angst as Cobain. On April 5, 1994, he took his own life.

Rock and Roll Enters Middle Age

The decade of the 1990s also saw the birth of a new style of rock known as alternative rock. Produced by minor labels—known as independents,

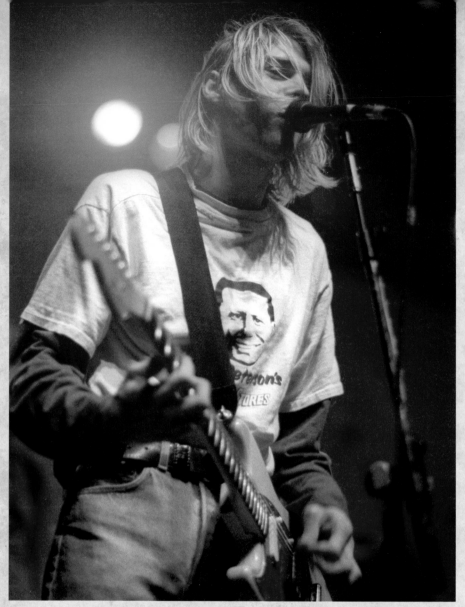

Nirvana's troubled singer and guitarist, Kurt Cobain, performs in 1993—just a few months before he committed suicide. Cobain and Nirvana's grunge rock fully captured the angst of Gen X.

or indies—these rock bands could usually be found in underground nightclubs near college campuses. In many cases the bands cut their own CDs and sold them at their shows. This style of rock tried to recapture the angry attitudes and metal sounds of the 1960s and 1970s rock groups that the indie performers believed had been lost due to the overcommercialization of rock and roll music that arrived in the music video era. Most of these groups had small and dedicated follow-ings, but some alternative rock groups did enjoy some breakout success. Among the more successful alternative rock bands of the 1990s were the Smashing Pumpkins, Red Hot Chili Peppers, Radiohead, Toad the Wet Sprocket, and Counting Crows.

If rock and roll was born in 1951 when Alan Freed first shouted "Go! Go! Gogogogogogogo!"[42] on the air, then rock turned fifty years old in 2001. Clearly, rock and roll has now entered middle age. The fact that Bruce Springsteen turned sixty-three in 2012 and yet continues to tour speaks volumes about his enduring appeal. Other veteran rockers continue to tour as well—in 2012 the Rolling Stones celebrated their fiftieth anniversary by playing to sold-out venues in London, New York City, and Newark, New Jersey. And the metal band Judas Priest toured in 2012 as well, visiting twenty-five European cities over the course of five weeks. Springsteen, the Stones, and Judas Priest illustrate the stay-ing power of rock and roll. Even though these rock acts have performed for decades, they are still widely popular as they tour and make new mu-sic, enabling new fans to discover their sounds while old fans stay loyal.

Chapter 5

What Is the Legacy of Rock and Roll?

The chart-topping songs of 1950 included the melancholy "Mona Lisa" by Nat "King" Cole, the country-and-western hit "Tennessee Waltz" by Patti Page, and the easy-listening standard "Goodnight, Irene" by the Weavers. These songs in the pre–rock and roll era told moody stories of romance. These songs and others were not written or performed to offend, and they often ended with the optimistic message that love would prevail.

Twenty years later the chart-topping songs included rock anthems such as "Mama Told Me Not to Come" by Three Dog Night, which described misadventures at a boozy party; "Let It Be," a call for world peace by the Beatles recorded during the height of the Vietnam War; and "He Ain't Heavy . . . He's My Brother," a song by the Hollies that delivered a message of hope that all people would join together in friendship.

Clearly, rock and roll changed popular music from what had been a light and family-oriented form of entertainment into a medium that could deliver strong social messages. Certainly, many rock and roll songs still dwell on romance, but the lyrics in rock music have often touched on the grittier side of love, and very often the songs have not ended on notes of optimism. Indeed, another top song of 1970 was "American Woman" by the Guess Who, in which the singer warns his girlfriend to stay away because he fears falling in love with her and would rather enjoy his freedom.

Thomas E. Larson, an author and professor of music at the University of Nebraska, says rock and roll reflects the true nature of people's feelings toward one another as well as their ideas about how society should be shaped. Before the emergence of rock and roll, Larson says, record company executives believed the way to sell records was to ensure the music would not offend listeners. Larson says rock and roll proves people want their music to reflect what life is really about. "When rock and roll exploded onto the American landscape in the mid-1950s, it marked nothing less than a defining moment in our history," says Larson. "Rock and roll is, simply stated, the music of the people. . . . For the first time in our history, the music of the streets and cities, of the underprivileged and disaffected, the angry and rebellious became America's popular music."[43]

Rock Remains Socially Relevant

That trend has continued into the twenty-first century as rock music still delivers socially relevant messages. Just as the rock and roll performers of the 1960s used their music as a voice to protest the war in Vietnam, rockers of the twenty-first century have also turned to music as a medium of protest. The Iraq War, for example, prompted music of protest from artists such as Josh Ritter ("Girl in the War" and "Thin Blue Flame"), Patti Smith ("Radio Baghdad"), and Arcade Fire ("Intervention"). Meanwhile, Bruce Springsteen has continued to make statements with his music. His 2012 album *Wrecking Ball* was embraced by the Occupy Wall Street movement because it spoke to the hardships of the 99 percent of Americans the Occupiers believe have not shared in the benefits of the American economy.

The ongoing popularity of rock and roll forced record executives to accept new content in songs, and it has also led them to accept new ways in which the music is produced. During the early days of rock and roll, bands often had to beg to get themselves noticed by record companies. In 1962 Brian Epstein, manager of the Beatles, convinced a talent scout from Decca to watch the band perform in a Liverpool nightclub, the Cavern Club. The talent scout liked what he saw and heard and invited the Beatles to record some demo tapes in the company's London studio. Ultimately, Decca elected not to sign the Beatles to a recording

Lyrics with political messages have long been a part of rock and roll, and that tradition continues. A 2012 Bruce Springsteen album spoke to the hardships of the 99 percent of Americans who have not, in the view of the Occupy Wall Street movement, shared in the benefits of the American economy. Occupy protesters march in New York in 2011.

contract. In fact, the head of Decca, Dick Rowe, told the Beatles' manager, "Guitar groups are on the way out, Mr. Epstein."[44]

The recording industry has changed since Decca turned down the Beatles. Most significantly, the Internet has enabled unknown bands to give rock fans a taste of their music. Using equipment and software available to any consumer, up-and-coming rock groups and other musicians can record their music, produce videos of their performances, and upload these images and sounds onto YouTube.

Discovered on the Internet

Some performers have posted their own websites while others use Facebook, Bebo, Hi5, and similar social networking sites that can display videos and play music. The young Canadian pop singer Justin Bieber serves as a prime example of a star discovered through the power of the Internet.

Bieber was discovered on YouTube by record producer Scott "Scooter" Braun in 2006, when Bieber was just twelve years old. Braun was trolling through YouTube when he stumbled across a video Bieber had uploaded of himself performing a song by the R&B artist Ne-Yo, recorded at a talent show in Stratford, Ontario. At the time, the Jonas Brothers had just exploded onto the pop scene, and Braun was in search of a performer who could appeal to the same audience—tween girls. "There is a place in the market for a kid with an angelic, soulful voice," Braun says. "I was like, 'This is the kid I've been looking for.'"[45] Under Braun's management, Bieber signed a recording contract with Island Def Jam, a label headed by the R&B star Usher.

Now Bieber is one of the hottest performers in popular music. And he has attained that status by relying heavily on the Internet to reach his fans. Bieber has his own YouTube channel, which by 2012 had garnered some 3 billion views. Also, in 2012 it was reported that he adds some forty-three thousand Twitter followers *a day*—giving him a direct pipeline to the young people who buy his music. Bieber is not regarded as a pure rock performer—his sound falls more into the genre of R&B. Nevertheless his success illustrates how the Internet has given him control of his career that he would never have had in the predigital age.

Journey Finds a New Star

Pure rock performers have also relied on the Internet to boost their careers. One performer whose Internet presence led to stardom is Arnel Pineda, a native of the Philippines, whose YouTube videos prompted the veteran rock band Journey to select him as its new lead singer. In fact, Journey had been without a regular lead singer since the 1990s, when Steve Perry left the band. Since then the band has used a number of singers. None were able to adequately fill Perry's role by giving voice to Journey's music, which requires a singer capable of hitting a wide range of notes.

And so Neal Schon, Journey's guitarist, spent hours in front of his computer screen, trolling through YouTube and other Internet sites in search of a new lead singer. Finally, in 2007 Schon came across a video

Canadian pop singer Justin Bieber (performing in 2012) is one of many new, young musicians who have been discovered through the power and reach of the Internet. Bieber's YouTube video attracted the attention of a record producer in 2006.

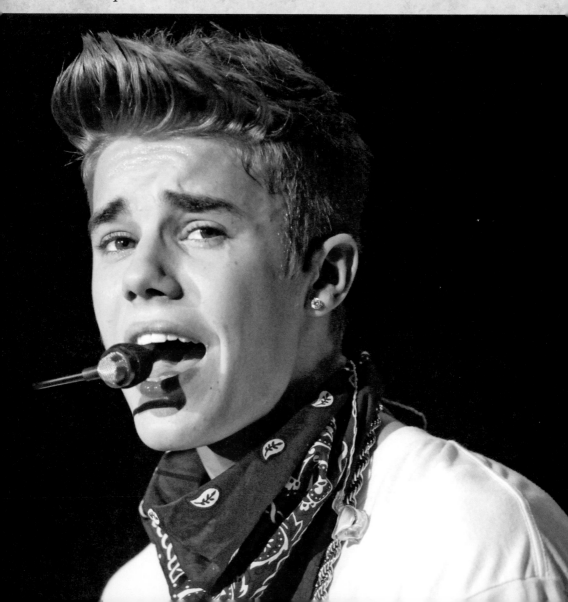

of Pineda performing in front of a Journey cover band in Manila, the Philippine capital.

"After watching the videos over and over again, I had to walk away from the computer and let what I heard sink in because it sounded too good to be true," recalls Schon. "I thought, 'He can't be that good.' I tried to get a hold of him and I finally heard from him that night, but it took some convincing to get him to believe that it really was me and not an impostor."[46] Schon convinced Pineda to fly to America for an audition, and after Schon's bandmates heard Pineda perform, he joined Journey as the group's new lead singer.

Propelling New Technologies

Clearly, rock and roll music has found a niche on the Internet, but it can be argued that rock has always enjoyed a close relationship with technology. Indeed, rock emerged as electrically amplified music that was made possible due to the development of the solid-body electric guitar, the invention of the transistor, and other advancements.

But it could also be argued that rock and roll provided the fuel that has driven the development of new technologies. Because of the overwhelming popularity of rock and roll, and the enormous profits at stake, electronics companies readily devoted their resources to developing new ways to listen to the music: transistor radios, eight-track tape players, portable tape and CD players, and eventually, the development of MP3 technology and the devices people use to listen to MP3 files.

Bono, lead singer for the rock group U2, believes the technological giants of the late twentieth century and early twenty-first century—people like Microsoft founders Paul Allen and Bill Gates and the late Steve Jobs, cofounder of Apple—were inspired to develop new technologies because of their appreciation for rock music. Says Bono:

The people who invented the 21st century had their consciousness shaped by music and by powerful rock and roll music, and it's not just Steve Jobs, it was Paul Allen, it was lots of people. I once put this to Bill Gates, I said, "I know you probably didn't

The Rock and Roll Hall of Fame

The significance of rock and roll in the American experience prompted leaders of the music industry to establish the Rock and Roll Hall of Fame in 1983. The 150,000-square-foot (13,936 sq. m) museum, which includes four theaters, is located in Cleveland, Ohio, the city where disc jockey Alan Freed first coined the term *rock and roll* as he spun records on *The Moondog Show* in 1951.

Since the museum opened, more than seven hundred performers have been inducted into the Hall of Fame. Many of the inductees are pure rockers, such as members of the Beatles and Rolling Stones, but performers from other genres of popular music have also been inducted. According to the Hall of Fame, voters consider "the influence and significance of the artists' contributions to the development and perpetuation of rock and roll" when deciding the eligibility of nominees for induction. Over the years, performers such as the Swedish pop group ABBA, R&B stars Gladys Knight and the Pips, punk rockers the Sex Pistols, and country rockers ZZ Top have been inducted.

Each year, more than six hundred performers, producers, record company executives, and other music industry insiders vote to induct nominees into the hall. Starting in 2012 the Hall of Fame also accepted ballots from fans, who could cast votes for nominees through *Rolling Stone* magazine's website, www.rollingstone.com.

Rock and Roll Hall of Fame, "Induction Process," 2012. http://rockhall.com.

listen to Jimi Hendrix," and Bill protested, "Are you kidding me, in all my time with Paul Allen, how could I have not been shaped by Jimi Hendrix? That's all we heard 10 hours a day."[47]

The Demise of the Record Store

Rock and roll may have helped propel the technological developments that enable its fans to listen to the music in new and innovative ways, but these innovations have also led to the demise of record stores. Since most music is now sold online as MP3 files or on CDs through Internet-based retailers such as Amazon—or in brick-and-mortar superstores such as Walmart and Best Buy—the neighborhood record stores have largely disappeared from American cities and towns.

When rock and roll first emerged in the 1950s, record stores were more than just places where people bought albums and 45s. Young people congregated in the stores after school to listen to vinyl records in private booths and talk with clerks and one another about their favorite bands. Now people can sample the music at Apple's iTunes online store or exchange their ideas about music through blogs. According to the group Record Collectors Guild—an organization for people who collect vintage recordings—fewer than five hundred record stores remain in business in America, and all of those are independently owned. The last major record chain, Tower Records, filed for bankruptcy in 2004 and eventually closed all its stores. Now Tower Records exists as an online retailer only. One independent store owner, Thom Spennato, owner of Sound Track in New York City, says most of his customers are middle-aged. "We don't see the kids anymore," he says. "The 12- to 15-year-old market, that what's missing the last couple of years."[48]

Rock critic Dave Marsh points out that not only did record stores give music fans opportunities to learn about the hottest new bands, they also occasionally gave future rock stars the opportunities to learn what type of sounds fans want to hear. Indeed, before rock guitarist and songwriter Jonathan Richman and singer Iggy Pop found stardom in rock music, they worked behind the counters at record stores. "It's part of the transmission of music," says Marsh, who says he became a fan of the psychedelic rockers the Fugs and progressive rockers Frank Zappa and the Mothers of Invention after first hearing their sounds in record stores. "It seems like you can't have a neighborhood without them."[49]

Crossover Appeal

The record stores may not be surviving, but one legacy of rock that has survived and prospered is the improvement in race relations that rock and roll helped to foster. Indeed, rock helped break down color barriers not only in music, but in American culture as a whole. Rock and roll arrived during an era in American society when African Americans and other minorities were demanding equal rights.

In 1954, the same year Bill Haley and the Comets released "Rock Around the Clock"—a song that drew heavily from the African American jump blues sound—the US Supreme Court issued its landmark ruling in the *Brown v. Board of Education* case, outlawing segregation in schools and other institutions in American life. A year later, when Rosa Parks refused to give up her seat to a white man on a bus in Montgomery, Alabama, sparking the Montgomery bus boycott, the African American rocker Chuck Berry released "Maybellene," which hit the top of the charts and made him into a big star. And in 1960, when four young black men sat down at a whites-only lunch counter in Greensboro, North Carolina, and demanded to be served, African American singer Chubby Checker recorded "The Twist."

The *Brown* decision, as well as the Parks and Greensboro incidents, prompted much hostility among white southerners—but many southern teenagers, as well as teenagers elsewhere in America, were more likely to accept African Americans as equals because they did not care who recorded rock and roll music. They just wanted to hear the sounds and own the music. That is why early black rockers such as Chuck Berry and Little Richard found crossover appeal and popularity among white audiences. Says Reebee Garofalo, professor of media studies at the University of Massachusetts, "The rebellious tone of this music mirrored the growing demand for political change."[50]

New Sounds Emerge

Since those early days of rock and roll, many black rockers have emerged, including Jimi Hendrix, Chubby Checker, and Jackie Wilson in the 1960s; Clarence Clemons, the sax player for the E Street Band in

The Beatles, Rolling Stones, Elvis Presley, Buddy Holly, and other early pioneers of rock may have laid the groundwork for the genre to become an institution in the music world, but none of those artists can lay claim to recording the best-selling rock album of all time. According to the website Ultimate-Guitar.com, an international online forum for rock enthusiasts, that honor belongs to the Australian hard rock band AC/DC, whose 1980 album *Back in Black* has sold more copies than any other rock album. According to Ultimate-Guitar.com, since its release, *Back in Black* has sold more than 49 million copies.

In a review of the album, *Rolling Stone* reported, "From the ominous tolling that opened 'Hells Bells' to a closing blast of defiance titled 'Rock and Roll Ain't Noise Pollution,' the ten songs on *Back in Black* rock out with brute force and raunchy humor."

According to Ultimate-Guitar.com, other top-selling rock albums include Pink Floyd's *Dark Side of the Moon*, 45 million; Meat Loaf's *Bat Out of Hell*, 43 million; Fleetwood Mac's *Rumors*, 40 million; Led Zeppelin's *Led Zeppelin IV*, 37 million; Alanis Morissette's *Jagged Little Pill*, 33 million; the Beatles' *Sgt. Pepper's Lonely Hearts Club Band*, 32 million; Nirvana's *Nevermind*, 30 million; Guns N' Roses' *Appetite for Destruction*, 28 million; and Santana's *Supernatural*, 27 million.

Rolling Stone, "AC/DC: *Back in Black*," November 16, 1989. www.rollingstone.com.

the 1970s; Prince in the 1980s; Lenny Kravitz in the 1990s; and since 2000, stars such as Howard Jones, former lead singer for Killswitch Engage and Blood Has Been Shed, and Byron Davis, vocalist for the metal band God Forbid.

As rock and roll moves further into the twenty-first century, many critics are unsure of how the sound will continue to develop. Many new bands have emerged since 2000; among the new breed of rockers are Mumford & Sons, Arcade Fire, Passion Pit, Muse, and the Black Keys. But many experts suggest that these bands and others have failed to carve out their own niche in the evolution of rock and roll—much as the folk rockers did in the 1960s, the punk rockers did in the 1970s, the music video stars did in the 1980s, and the grunge bands did in the 1990s. Instead, the bands of today have built on the sounds pioneered by others.

Experts such as George Ergatoudis, an executive with the British Broadcasting Corporation, maintain that new trends in rock will emerge. Ergatoudis points out that since its inception, rock has depended largely on the talents of its guitarists. Perhaps a new sound that does not rely on guitar riffs needs to be introduced into rock, he says. Ergatoudis points to the trend in electronic dance music, also known as electronica, synth house, and electro house. He says the success of Canadian Joel Zimmerman, who performs under the name deadmau5 (pronounced "dead mouse"), may provide an indication of where rock is heading. Deadmau5 concocts his beats electronically through computers, drumbeat machines, and other synthesizers. The large crowds that flock to his shows illustrate that fans may be willing to accept music without guitars. Kerri Mason, a dance writer for *Billboard*, adds that electronic dance music may mean "the death of the guitar and the rise of the laptop" when it comes to making music. She adds, "It's a huge wave, and it's not slowing down. I don't think we've seen its peak yet, not that massive moment of crossover."[51]

Others disagree, maintaining that rock and roll is not rock and roll without the sound of the electric guitar. New artists will emerge, promises Foo Fighters guitarist Dave Grohl, and they will introduce new sounds into the genre. "I just want to say: Never lose faith in real rock and roll music, you know what I mean? Never lose faith in that," says Grohl. "You might have to look a little harder, but it's always going to be there."[52]

Over the years, rock and roll has progressed from the sounds of Ike Turner, Bill Haley, and Buddy Holly in the 1950s; the British Invasion bands, folk rockers, acid rockers, and surf bands of the 1960s; the punks, glam rockers, and metal bands of the 1970s; the video stars of the 1980s; and the grunge bands of the 1990s. Throughout the rock and roll era, the music has always found a way to stay relevant and popular among fans. And Grohl is not the first rocker to predict that rock and roll will endure. In fact, that prediction was first made as far back as 1958 by the doo wop group Danny and the Juniors when they released their hit song "Rock and Roll Is Here to Stay."

Source Notes

Introduction: The Defining Characteristics of Rock and Roll

1. Quoted in David Remnick, "We Are Alive," *New Yorker*, July 30, 2012, p. 40.
2. Roberto Avant-Mier, *Rock the Nation: Latin/o Identities and the Latin Rock Diaspora*. New York: Continuum International, 2010, pp. 23–24.
3. Quoted in Cameron Crowe, "5 Against the World," *Rolling Stone*, October 28, 1993, p. 50.
4. Quoted in Ed Ward, Geoffrey Stokes, and Ken Tucker, *Rock of Ages: The Rolling Stone History of Rock & Roll*. New York: Rolling Stone, 1986, pp. 13–14.

Chapter One: What Conditions Led to the Birth of Rock and Roll?

5. Quoted in Ward, Stokes, and Tucker, *Rock of Ages*, p. 68.
6. Quoted in Ward, Stokes, and Tucker, *Rock of Ages*, p. 69.
7. Quoted in Ward, Stokes, and Tucker, *Rock of Ages*, p. 70.
8. Quoted in Preston Lauterbach, *The Chitlin' Circuit: And the Road to Rock 'n' Roll*. New York: W.W. Norton, 2011, p. 11.
9. Quoted in Gerri Hirshey, "Pink Cadillacs, Little Red Corvettes: Paradise by the Dashboard Light," *Rolling Stone*, May 11, 2000, p. 87.
10. David Fricke, "Introduction *to Rolling Stone*'s 100 Greatest Guitarists of All Time," *Rolling Stone Special Edition*, 2012, p. 7.
11. Quoted in Jon Pareles, "Les Paul, Wizard of the Electric Guitar and Recording Studio, Dies at 94," *New York Times*, August 14, 2009, p. B14.

12. Quoted in *Music Trades*, "Les Paul and How He Shaped the Industry," October 2009, p. 106.
13. André Millard, *The Electric Guitar: A History of an American Icon*. Baltimore: Johns Hopkins University Press, 2004, p. 6.
14. Jim Dawson, *Rock Around the Clock: The Record That Started the Rock Revolution*. San Francisco: Backbeat, 2005, p. 6.

Chapter Two: Rockabilly, Duck Walking, and the Death of Buddy Holly

15. Wally George, "Elvis Wriggles, Fans Scream at Pan-Pacific," *Los Angeles Times*, October 29, 1957, p. C8.
16. Quoted in Glenn C. Altschuler, *All Shook Up: How Rock 'n' Roll Changed America*. New York: Oxford University Press, 2004, pp. 29–30.
17. Quoted in Altschuler, *All Shook Up*, p. 30.
18. Quoted in H. Allen Smith, "A Crooner Comes Back," *Saturday Evening Post*, August 31, 1957, p. 68.
19. Quoted in Pete Martin, "I Call on Bing Crosby," *Saturday Evening Post*, May 11, 1957, p. 119.
20. Quoted in Irwin Stambler, *The Encyclopedia of Pop, Rock and Soul*, rev. ed. New York: St. Martin's, 1989, p. 411.
21. Quoted in Michael Seth Starr, *Bobby Darin: A Life*. Lanham, MD: Taylor Trade, 2004, pp. 31–32.
22. Bruce Eder, "Buddy Holly," AllMusic, 2012. www.allmusic.com.

Chapter Three: The 1960s Rock Metamorphosis

23. Quoted in Lloyd Shearer, "What Do You Think of the Twist?," *Boston Globe*, February 18, 1962, p. B6.
24. Quoted in *Ebony*, "Chubby Checker: Singer Sparks 'Twist' Craze," January 1961, p. 41.
25. Quoted in Matthew F. Delmont, *The Nicest Kids in Town: American Bandstand, Rock 'n' Roll and the Struggle for Civil Rights in 1950s Philadelphia*. Berkeley: University of California Press, 2012, p. 168.

26. Quoted in Dan Deluca, "Chubby Checker, Dick Clark and 'The Twist,'" *Philadelphia Inquirer*, April 18, 2012. www.philly.com.

27. Murray Schumach, "The Sky Glows over Queens as the Beatles Take Over Shea Stadium," *New York Times*, August 16, 1965, p. 29.

28. *New York Times*, "Beatles Make Long Hairs of 9- to 12-Year-Old Set," October 14, 1963, p. 54.

29. Mopsy Strange Kennedy, "Put Another Record on the Pornograph," *Los Angeles Times*, July 23, 1967, p. C1.

30. Quoted in Irwin Stambler, *The Encyclopedia of Pop, Rock, and Soul*, p. 581.

31. Lindsey Buckingham, "100 Greatest Artists: The Beach Boys," *Rolling Stone*, 2013, www.rollingstone.com.

32. Quoted in Andy Greene, "Exclusive Q&A: Original Beach Boy David Marks on the Band's Anniversary Tour," *Rolling Stone*, March 16, 2012, www.rollingstone.com.

33. Buckingham, "100 Greatest Artists: The Beach Boys."

34. Mikal Gilmore, "Sixties," *Rolling Stone*, August 23, 1990, p. 61.

Chapter Four: Rock Enters the Video Age

35. Richard Cromelin, "Devo Veers from Chaos to Clarity," *Los Angeles Times*, October 11, 1978, p. F10.

36. Quoted in History.com, "MTV Launches," 2012. www.history.com.

37. Quoted in Greg Prato, *MTV Ruled the World: The Early Years of Music Video*. London: Lulu, 2010, p. 33.

38. Quoted in Tom King, *Metallica: Uncensored on the Record*. Warwickshire, England: Coda, 2011, ebook.

39. Roger Sabin, *Punk Rock: So What?* New York: Routledge, 1999, pp. 2–3.

40. Quoted in Robert Palmer, "Emerson, Lake and Palmer Go Classical," *New York Times*, July 8, 1977, p. 51.

41. Latoya Peterson, "Where Did Our Angst Go? Teen Esprit Revisited," *Spin*, August 1, 2011. www.spin.com.

42. Quoted in Ward, Stokes and Tucker, *Rock of Ages*, p. 70.

Chapter Five: What Is the Legacy of Rock and Roll?

43. Thomas E. Larson, *History of Rock and Roll*. Dubuque, IA: Kendall Hunt, 2004, p. 2.

44. Quoted in Bryan Roylance, Julian Quance, Oliver Craske, and Roman Milisic, eds., *The Beatles Anthology*. San Francisco: Chronicle, 2000, p. 67.

45. Quoted in Lizzie Widdicombe, "Teen Titan: The Man Who Made Justin Bieber," *New Yorker*, September 3, 2012, p. 53.

46. Quoted in Ramona S. Diaz, "Don't Stop Believin': Everyman's Journey," 2012. http://everymansjourney.com.

47. Quoted in Brian Hiatt, "Exclusive Q&A: Bono on Steve Jobs' Rock and Roll Spirit," *Rolling Stone*, October 7, 2011. www.rollingstone.com.

48. Quoted in Alex Williams, "The Graying of the Record Store," *New York Times*, July 16, 2006. www.nytimes.com.

49. Quoted in Williams, "The Graying of the Record Store."

50. Reebee Garofalo, *Rockin' the Boat: Mass Music and Mass Movements*. Cambridge, MA: South End, 1992, p. 232.

51. Quoted in Edna Gundersen, "Deadmau5 Is More EDM Showman than DJ," *USA Today*, September 11, 2005, p. 1D.

52. Quoted in Gazelle Emami, "Is Rock Music Dead? Not If Dave Grohl Has Anything to Say About It," *Huffington Post*, February 13, 2012. www.huffingtonpost.com.

Important People in the History of Rock and Roll

The Beatles: British rockers John Lennon, Paul McCartney, George Harrison, and Ringo Starr hit stardom in 1963 with the album *Please Please Me* and then led the British Invasion when they appeared on the *Ed Sullian Show* in 1964. The band broke up in 1970. Lennon was killed by a deranged fan in 1980; Harrison died of cancer in 2001.

Chuck Berry: One of the first African American rock and roll stars, Berry proved that rock has crossover appeal and is capable of finding fans of all races. In 1955 he recorded the hit "Maybellene" and proved that stage presence is also an important aspect of rock.

The Buggles: Trevor Horne and Geoff Downes, members of the short-lived New Wave rock group, recorded a modestly successful single titled "Video Killed the Radio Star," but the video they made of the song was featured in 1981 when MTV launched its first day on the air.

Chubby Checker: Checker recorded "The Twist" in 1960, establishing the twist as the first successful dance to emerge out of rock and roll music.

Dick Clark: Clark served as host of *American Bandstand* for most of the show's run on national TV, from 1952 through 1988. Clark used the show to introduce teenagers to many new and established rock and roll stars.

Kurt Cobain: Cobain and his band, Nirvana, were the most successful of the grunge rockers, whose songs reflected the angst of young people who entered their teenage and adult years in the 1990s.

Alan Freed: Starting in 1951 Freed played jump blues on his radio program, *The Moondog Show*; he coined the term *rock and roll* and became an influential figure in rock and roll music.

Bill Haley: Haley and his band, the Comets, recorded the first major rock and roll hits, "Shake, Rattle & Roll" and "Rock Around the Clock," the second of which spent eight weeks in 1955 at the top of the *Billboard* magazine pop music chart.

Les Paul: Paul invented the electric guitar in 1929 when he jammed a phonograph needle into his acoustic guitar below the strings to amplify the music so it could be heard over a noisy barroom crowd. In 1941 he developed the first solid-body electric guitar—a design that is still in use today.

Sam Phillips: The founder of Sun Records, Phillips recorded "Rocket 88" and later developed the rockabilly sound, a hybrid of country-and-western and R&B played to a rock and roll beat. Among the stars he discovered were Elvis Presley, Jerry Lee Lewis, Roy Orbison, and Carl Perkins.

Elvis Presley: Rock and roll's first superstar, Presley was discovered by Sun Records in 1953. He brought sex appeal to his performances, mostly by swinging his hips in a suggestive manner. Presley eventually sold more than 77 million records. He died in 1977 at age forty-two from an irregular heartbeat caused by the abuse of prescription drugs.

Sex Pistols: The group consisting of John Lydon (Johnny Rotten), John Ritchie (Sid Vicious), Steve Jones, and Paul Cook rose to the top of the punk rock movement in the 1970s as they found an audience for their vulgar, antiestablishment music.

Ed Sullivan: Sullivan hosted a popular TV variety show in the 1950s and 1960s. He is responsible for introducing Americans to major rock and roll stars, including Elvis Presley, the Beatles, the Rolling Stones, Chubby Checker, the Doors, and the Mamas and the Papas.

Ike Turner: Turner's band, Kings of Rhythm, recorded "Rocket 88" in 1951; it is regarded as the first true rock and roll song.

For Further Research

Books

Daniel Bukszpan, *The Encyclopedia of Heavy Metal.* Toronto: Sterling, 2012.

Marc Dolan, *Bruce Springsteen and the Promise of Rock 'n' Roll.* New York: Norton, 2012.

Michael Dregni, *Rockabilly: The Twang Heard 'Round the World.* Minneapolis: Voyageur, 2011.

Mike Evans and Paul Kingsbury, eds., *Woodstock: Three Days That Rocked the World.* Toronto: Sterling, 2010.

Otto Fuchs, *Bill Haley: Father of Rock 'n' Roll.* Gelnhausen, Germany: Wagner, 2011.

Jeff Gold, *101 Essential Rock Records.* Berkeley, CA: Gingko, 2012.

Dave Hunter, *The Fender Telecaster: The Life and Times of the Electric Guitar That Changed the World.* Minneapolis: Voyageur, 2012.

Craig Marks and Rob Tannenbaum, *I Want My MTV: The Uncensored Story of the Music Video Revolution.* New York: Dutton, 2011.

Keith Richards, *Life.* New York: Little, Brown, 2010.

Raymond I. Schuck, ed., *Do You Believe in Rock and Roll? Essays on Don Mclean's "American Pie."* Jefferson, NC: McFarland, 2012.

Websites

American Masters: Les Paul (www.pbs.org/wnet/americanmasters/episodes/les-paul/chasing-sound/100). Companion website to the August 13, 2009, PBS show *American Masters* episode devoted to the life and career of Les Paul, inventor of the electric guitar. Students can find a transcript of the show, photographs of Paul, and a timeline of important dates in the life of Paul and his work to perfect the sound of the electric guitar.

The Ed Sullivan Show (www.edsullivan.com). Ed Sullivan hosted a national TV variety show that helped introduce rock and roll to millions of viewers. Visitors to the show's website can access pages devoted to the appearances on Sullivan's show by Elvis Presley, the Beatles, the Rolling Stones, the Doors, and the Mamas and the Papas. Included on the pages are videos of the performers' appearances on the show.

Elvis Presley: Official Site of the King of Rock 'n' Roll (www.elvis .com). This site is maintained by the estate of Elvis Presley and includes a biography of rock and roll's first superstar as well as a list of his albums and singles. Fans can also find an overview of his acting career that chronicles his film roles. By following the link to Graceland, fans can see photos, updated every sixty seconds, of the scene outside Presley's mansion in Memphis, Tennessee.

Joe Smith Collection at the Library of Congress (www.loc.gov/rr/record/joesmith). Longtime record company executive Joe Smith created an oral history of popular music, taping performers and other music industry insiders discussing their lives and what led them to make music. Smith donated his collection to the Library of Congress. Students can access recordings made of Les Paul, George Harrison, Mick Jagger, and other pioneers of rock and roll.

Museum of Broadcast Communications: *American Bandstand* (www .museum.tv/eotvsection.php?entrycode=americanband). The Chicago-based museum maintains a history of the popular dance show that remained on the air from 1952 through 1988, introducing many teenagers to new as well as established rock and roll stars. Students can read a history of the show and also find a link to a biography of Dick Clark, who hosted *American Bandstand* for most of its thirty-six-year history.

Radio Hall of Fame: Alan Freed (www.radiohof.org/discjockey/alan freed.html). Despite his conviction in the payola scandal, Alan Freed was inducted into the National Radio Hall of Fame in 1988 for his contributions to the promotion of rock and roll. Visitors to the organization's website can read a biography of Freed and access a recording of his show. The Hall of Fame is housed in a wing of the Chicago-based Museum of Broadcast Communications.

Rock and Roll Hall of Fame (http://rockhall.com). The Rock and Roll Hall of Fame has inducted more than seven hundred performers and other music industry insiders who have contributed to the development of rock music. Visitors to the website can read biographies of the inductees and access photographs of the hall's exhibits. By following the "Archives" link, students can find numerous articles on rock and roll history.

Rolling Stone (www.rollingstone.com). Official website of the magazine that has chronicled rock and roll as well as other forms of popular music since the publication was founded in 1967 by Jann Wenner. The magazine has made an extensive archive of its articles available online. Students can find many resources about performers and trends in music by accessing the site's search engine.

Index

Note: boldface page numbers indicate illustrations.

Picture Credits

Cover: Thinkstock Images

AP Images: 70

© Bettmann/Corbis: 47, 59

© Kevin P. Casey/Corbis: 66

© Robb Cohen/Retna Ltd./Corbis: 72

© Dieter Klar/dpa/Corbis: 53

© Elliot Landy/Corbis: 51

© Ross Marino/Sygma/Corbis: 12

Photofest: 37

Steph/Visual/ZumaPress/Newscom: 17

© Benoit Tessier/Reuters/Corbis: 25

Thinkstock Images: 8, 9

© ullstein bild/AP/Corbis: 30

About the Author

Hal Marcovitz is a former newspaper reporter and the author of more than 150 books for young readers. His other titles in the Understanding American History series include *The 1960s* and *The Roaring Twenties*. He makes his home in Chalfont, Pennsylvania.